The *little* Big Book of

WORLD CUP
CRICKET

The *little* Big Book of
WORLD CUP
CRICKET

Indra Vikram Singh

media Eight

Published in 2011 by

Media Eight Publishing
India Private Limited

302-A, ABW Tower, M G Road
Gurgaon 122001, India
Tel: 0124 4040017

ISBN: 9788173142208

Printed in India

To,

Joey

for a glorious innings

with a straight bat

Contents

Acknowledgements

I acknowledge with deep gratitude the assistance received from officials of the International Cricket Council (ICC), ICC World Cup 2003 secretariat, Marylebone Cricket Club (MCC), Bangladesh Cricket Board, Canadian Cricket Association, Kenya Cricket Association, Zimbabwe Cricket Union, Wisden Cricketers' Almanac, Mr. Matthew Engel, Ms. Harriet Monkhouse, Mr. Brijmohan Singh, and my son Vishvajeet. I am also honoured that Mr. Ajay Parmar and Media Eight found the first edition of my book good enough to be published in this new, attractive format.

Preface

This is the second, updated and abridged edition of The Little Big Book of World Cup Cricket which was originally published in 2007. Media Eight decided to publish a leaner and attractive edition in the run-up to the ICC World Cup 2011. The book is a story of the cricket World Cup from its inception in 1975, through all the nine editions up to 2007, and carries a preview of the 2011 event. It includes all the highlights, the great matches, brilliant individual performances, the icons who dazzled and detailed records. Everything noteworthy has been incorporated in a manner that the cricket fan can breeze through the greatest event in the One-day game as it unfolded over the last three-and-a-half decades.

One can see the game evolving from its traditional form to assume a modern avatar embracing night matches, coloured clothing and technology. While the run-rates have climbed, bowlers have innovated to produce deliveries meant to stifle big-hitting, and fielding standards have hit new highs. I earnestly hope you will all enjoy reading the book as much as I have been delighted in writing and compiling it.

September 13, 2010 **Indra Vikram Singh**

The Cricket World Cup

1975

The International Cricket Conference (ICC), now known as International Cricket Council, approved a proposal on 25 July 1973 to hold a Limited-overs World Cup tournament. Hardly could anyone have imagined what a mega event this would become right from its inception.

When the World Cup first began in 1975, scarcely two years before the centenary of Test matches, One-day cricket was a vastly different game. There were no fielding circles, white balls, coloured clothing or helmets. Most of the teams had little experience in this form of the game; just 18 One-day Internationals had been played till then. Only the English players - and the overseas professionals - had received adequate exposure in the truncated game on the county circuit.

The Prudential Assurance Company pitched in with sponsorship worth £100,000 ($162,000) and the tournament got under way amid great euphoria. How much excitement there was, could be gauged from the fact that Sir Garfield Sobers, inarguably the greatest allround cricketer ever, was initially included in the West Indies squad even though it was known that a debilitating knee injury had effectively finished his career. That the mighty Sobers was unable to participate is another matter.

England, long considered the home of cricket with headquarters at Lord's, was deemed to be a natural venue for the World Cup. Long hours of daylight and several top-class grounds located not far from each other were cited as factors in favour of retaining England as the permanent base for the premier event. It did not take long for the players, public or administrators to realise that they had a product that was an instant hit.

The first tournament was played for an exquisite sterling silver trophy, 18.5 inches high and containing 89.5 ounces of the sparkling metal. Never before had there been such a large and distinguished gathering of the world's finest cricketers.

There were six Test-playing countries then: Australia, England, India, New Zealand, Pakistan and the West Indies. To this list were added Sri Lanka, for long a strong contender for Test status, and East Africa, considered the best of the rest. The teams were divided into two groups. In Group A were East Africa, England, India and New Zealand. Group B comprised Australia, Pakistan, Sri Lanka and the West Indies. In the semi-finals Australia beat England, and the West Indies trounced New Zealand.

The West Indies, then beginning their ascent to the pinnacle with an incredible run of successes, won the inaugural Prudential World Cup final. There was tremendous Caribbean support at Lord's on that grand occasion as 26,000 spectators sat enthralled till 8-45 in the evening, watching the drama unfold. It was a box-office bonanza too, with £66,400 in the kitty, considered a world record at the time for a day's collection in a Limited-overs match.

The total prize money on offer was £9,000, with the winners receiving £4,000 along with gilt silver medals for each player. The runners-up got £2,000, and the losing semi-finalists £1,000 each. Total gate money of £188,598 was paid by the 158,000 people who came in through the turnstiles. A profit of £200,000 provided ample indication that the event had enormous potential to generate hitherto unimagined revenue for the game.

The World Cup became a great spectacle, graced by princes and prime ministers, and savoured by a huge number of people all over the globe.

The final:

Lord's, London, 21 June 1975

West Indies won by 17 runs

West Indies: *291 for 8 wickets in 60 overs (Rohan Kanhai 55, Clive Lloyd 102, Keith Boyce 34, Gary Gilmour 5 for 48)*

Australia: *274 all out in 58.4 overs (Alan Turner 40, Ian Chappell 62, Doug Walters 35, Keith Boyce 4 for 50)*

Man of the Match: Clive Lloyd

1979

There was little change in 1979, with the same venue, the same sponsor doling out two-and-a-half times the amount given previously, and the same winner. The one difference was that a tournament for the associate members was conducted earlier, and the winners Sri Lanka and runners-up Canada, earned the right to participate in the World Cup alongside the six Test-playing countries.

The second Prudential World Cup was played in the shadow of the crisis precipitated by the rebel World Series Cricket of Australian tycoon, Kerry Packer. He had contracted a number of top players of the world. The Australians and English did not include these players in the World Cup squads, though the West Indies and Pakistani Boards were not so harsh.

With the sponsorship amount at £250,000 ($405,000), the prize money was hiked to £25,900. The winners received £10,000, and the runners-up £4,000. The losing semi-finalists got £2,000 each. Inclement weather, which also led to the abandonment of a match, limited the crowds to 132,768 people, though the gate money nearly doubled to £359,717.

Group A now comprised Australia, Canada, England and Pakistan. In Group B were India, New Zealand, Sri Lanka and the West Indies. In the semi-finals, the West Indies defeated Pakistan, while England beat New Zealand.

The final:

Lord's, London, 23 June 1979

West Indies won by 92 runs

West Indies: *286 for 9 wickets in 60 overs (Vivian Richards 138 not out, Collis King 86)*

England: *194 all out in 51 overs (Mike Brearley 64, Geoff Boycott 57, Graham Gooch 32, Colin Croft 3 for 42, Joel Garner 5 for 38)*

Man of the Match: Vivian Richards

1983

In 1983, it was an enlarged format with each team playing the other twice in the respective groups. By now Sri Lanka had earned full membership of the ICC. Zimbabwe had emerged as the strongest outfit among the associate members, winning the ICC Trophy in 1982 easily.

Prudential continued to back the effort, raising the sponsorship figure to £500,000 ($810,000). Prize money went up to £66,200. The winners pocketed £20,000, while the runners-up got £8,000. The losing semi-finalists received £4,000 each. The crowds swelled to 232,081, the collections being £1,195,712. Guarantee money was paid for the first time, each Test-playing country receiving £53,900, and Zimbabwe £30,200. In addition, a surplus of £1 million was distributed among the teams.

In Group A this time were England, New Zealand, Pakistan

and Sri Lanka. Group B had Australia, India, the West Indies and Zimbabwe. In the semi-finals the West Indies beat Pakistan, while India defeated hosts England. Then, in one of the most stunning upsets in history, India trounced the West Indies to lift the third Prudential World Cup.

The final:

Lord's, London, 25 June 1983

India won by 43 runs

India: *183 all out in 54.4 overs (Krishnamachari Srikkanth 38, Andy Roberts 3 for 32)*

West Indies: *140 all out in 52 overs (Vivian Richards 33, Madan Lal 3 for 31, Mohinder Amarnath 3 for 12)*

Man of the Match: Mohinder Amarnath

1987

India's surprise win in 1983 strengthened the claims of the sub-continent to stage the event. The cricketing world thus travelled to a new destination in 1987, with India and Pakistan jointly hosting the event. The sponsorship also changed hands with Reliance Industries underwriting the effort. There was a new trophy too, a gold-plated cup, studded at the top with diamonds, and flags of all the participating nations embossed all round. It was crafted by Arun Industries of Jaipur and cost

Rs.600,000 ($42,260).

The sponsorship amount was about Rupees fifty million (£2.17 million), inclusive of title sponsorship, in-stadia advertising and merchandising rights. The prize money increased to £99,300 ($160,000), with the winners receiving £30,000 and the runners-up £12,000. The losing semi-finalists got £6,000 each. The guarantee money this time was £200,000 to Test-playing countries, and £170,000 to Zimbabwe. Amazing, though, it may seem today, Doordarshan paid nothing for television rights. Still, the gross earnings from the tournament were estimated to be $12 million.

With shorter hours of daylight during the northern winter, the number of overs to be bowled per innings was curtailed from 60, which was the norm in the first three World Cups, to 50. Innings of 50 overs came to be accepted universally thereafter in One-day matches. In Group A were Australia, India, New Zealand and Zimbabwe, who had qualified by winning the ICC Trophy for the second successive time in 1986. Group B comprised England, Pakistan, Sri Lanka and the West Indies.

The sentimental favourites were India and Pakistan, but both were upset in the semi-finals. First Australia defeated Pakistan, and next day England beat India. The final between the Ashes rivals was a keen affair. Australia narrowly beat England to lift the Reliance World Cup and signal their climb towards new peaks in world cricket.

The final:

Eden Gardens, Calcutta, 8 November 1987

Australia won by 7 runs

Australia: *253 for 5 wickets in 50 overs (David Boon 75, Dean Jones 33, Allan Border 31, Mike Veletta 45 not out)*

England: *246 for 8 wickets in 50 overs (Graham Gooch 35, Bill Athey 58, Mike Gatting 41, Allan Lamb 45)*

Man of the Match: David Boon

1992

Post-Packer Australia was fast establishing itself as the modern abode of the game. In addition, if India's triumph paved the way for staging the next tournament at their shores, Australia could not be denied the same right after their own day of glory at Calcutta in 1987. New Zealand shared the honour of hosting the show. Benson and Hedges sponsored the tournament this time, paying $5 million.

That cricket had finally emerged from its cocoon of conservatism was in stark evidence as the players pranced around at night in colourful outfits under the dazzling lights of Perth, Sydney and Melbourne. A sparkling globe of Waterford crystal costing $15,000, and mounted on a base embellished with nine medals displaying the coat of arms of the competing teams, replaced the traditional silver (or gold) cup. It was Pakistan's turn to claim the coveted prize.

A shrewd marketing blitz was launched, and there was a slew of official sponsors including Tyrell's wine. Kookaburra supplied the white balls and the largest assortment of coloured pads ever to be on show. Put on sale was a special collection of coins priced at over 1.71 million Australian dollars ($1.13 million), in sterling silver and 18-carat gold, with the World Cup engraved on them. These were similar to the nine medals mounted on the base of the trophy. There were 5,000 such sterling silver and 19 gold World Cup coin sets issued for souvenir hunters. The silver sets cost Aus $365 each, while the gold ones were priced at Aus $4510.

The prize money increased to Aus $290,000 ($191,000). The winners received Aus $50,000, the runners-up Aus $25,000, and the losing semi-finalists Aus $12,500 each. This time there was a prize awarded to the man-of-the-tournament, called world champion, worth Aus $5,000 plus a Nissan 300 car. It was won by New Zealand skipper Martin Crowe. The guarantee money paid to the nine teams was Aus $200,000 each.

The South Africans were welcomed back into the fold. With Zimbabwe - who lifted the ICC Trophy yet again in 1990 - too gaining full membership, this was the only occasion when the World Cup was contested by the Test-playing countries only. All the nine teams played each other in a round-robin league. It was in many ways a tournament of upsets. None of the three past champions – West Indies, India and Australia - made it to the semi-finals. Instead it was New Zealand who had a dream run of seven consecutive wins, before they crashed in the last two matches, including the semi-final. South Africa too surprised by quickly finding their feet on their return to international cricket after 21 years. They too made it to the semi-finals.

There was, however, some controversy over the rule for re-calculation of the target in rain-interrupted matches, whereby the highest-scoring overs of the team batting first were taken into consideration. As a result, there were instances when the target scores were not reduced by much, even as the number of balls to be faced were curtailed by a large number. The South Africans were victims of this in their semi-final against England.

The two finalists were England and Pakistan. For England it was the third final. Pakistan made their maiden entry, and they lifted the trophy in this new-look tournament. The traditional game had at last bridged the schism with the modern world.

The final:

MCG, Melbourne, 25 March 1992

Pakistan won by 22 runs

Pakistan: *249 for 6 wickets in 50 overs (Imran Khan 72, Javed Miandad 58, Inzamam-ul-Haq 42, Wasim Akram 33, Derek Pringle 3 for 22)*

England: *227 all out in 49.2 overs (Neil Fairbrother 62, Allan Lamb 31, Wasim Akram 3 for 49, Mushtaq Ahmed 3 for 41)*

Man of the Match: Wasim Akram

Player of the Tournament (World Champion): Martin Crowe

1996

The sub-continent had the honour of staging the tournament once again in 1996. This time three nations - India, Pakistan and Sri Lanka - played host. Now the top three associate members vied with nine teams from the big league. For the first time teams like ICC Trophy 1994 winners United Arab Emirates, Holland and Kenya made their appearance. Kenya had been represented in 1975 in the East Africa team. Now they were an entity by themselves.

Wills were the sponsors of this edition. The amount paid by them for title sponsorship only was Rupees 552 million ($12.8 million). It was cricketing heritage to the fore with a 28-inch sterling silver trophy, conceived and designed in 1882 specifically for the game of cricket by the 200-year-old Garrard and Company of London, the Crown jewellers. The trophy has etchings of a painting done in 1785 depicting a cricket match in progress. The painting adorns a wall of the cricket museum at Lord's.

That Sri Lanka, a team listed along with the minnows not long ago, lifted the exquisite trophy in a masterly display at Lahore, was evidence of the fact that the game had touched new frontiers.

The mascot for the tournament was an animated cricket ball named "Googlee", designed by Hindustan Thompson Associates. The sponsors described the mascot as a "reflection of the refreshing resurgence of a fine cricketing art - leg-spin bowling - within which the googly is the perfect symbol for intrigue, unpredictability, and the courage to dare to be different."

By now satellite television had ensured that cricket became a global sport. Unimagined sums were raked in by way of television rights, to vie with gate money in the revenue stakes. It was estimated that two million people watched the matches at the grounds, but two billion saw them on television during the 1996 World Cup, a quarter of these in India alone. No wonder World Tel paid $10.7 million plus 75 percent of the profits, totalling $22 million, for worldwide television rights that they in turn sold to various channels.

Instadia advertising rights were bought by Gokul Finance for Rs.150 million ($4 million). Professional Managment Group (PMG) helped sell these advertisement boards. Sightscreens and other instadia advertisements raked in another $1.5 million. The average gate collections are believed to have been around Rupees 10 million ($267,000) per match.

Marketing of the World Cup soared to amazing peaks. The official suppliers reportedly paid $8 million, with Coca Cola pouring in $3.7 million plus $340,000 for hoardings. Visa, Wimpy's and Indian Overseas Bank paid $350,000 each. Others like Taj Group of Hotels, Indian Airlines, Tradewings, PCL Computers and Fuji Film offered various packages. International Management Group (IMG) shelled out $4 million for hospitality tents that they put up in 17 venues across India. The prize money totalled £200,000 ($324,000), with the winners receiving £30,000 ($48,600), and the runners-up £20,000 ($32,400). The losing

The Cricket World Cup

semi-finalists received £10,000 ($16,200) each, while the losing quarter-finalists took home £5,000 ($8,100) each. The award for the man-of-the-tournament was an Audi A4 car, which was won by Sri Lanka's scintillating opening batsman Sanath Jayasuriya. Guarantee money of $405,000 each was paid to Test-playing nations, and $202,500 each to associate members. Even associate members that did not play this tournament received $162,000 each.

The teams were again divided into two groups. Group A comprised Australia, India, Kenya, Sri Lanka, West Indies and Zimbabwe. In Group B were England, Holland, New Zealand, Pakistan, South Africa and the United Arab Emirates. For the first time there was a quarter-final stage, and the teams that did not make it were Holland, Kenya, the United Arab Emirates and Zimbabwe. The semi-finals were contested between Australia and the West Indies, and India and Sri Lanka. Australia advanced to the final along with Sri Lanka, and the rest is history.

The final: *Gaddafi Stadium, Lahore, 17 March 1996*

Sri Lanka won by 7 wickets

Australia: *241 for 7 wickets in 50 overs (Mark Taylor 74, Ricky Ponting 45, Michael Bevan 36 not out, Aravinda de Silva 3 for 42)*

Sri Lanka: *245 for 3 wickets in 46.2 overs (Asanka Gurusinha 65, Aravinda de Silva 107 not out, Arjuna Ranatunga 47 not out)*

Man of the Match: Aravinda de Silva

Player of the Tournament: Sanath Jayasuriya

1999

The World Cup returned to England in 1999 after a lapse of 16 years. In keeping with the times, Holland and Ireland too got to host a match each, besides Scotland and Wales. So much had changed in the interim. An Indian businessman, Jagmohan Dalmiya, presided over the ICC after a stint by a great West Indies batsman of yore, Clyde Walcott.

Even the Marylebone Cricket Club (MCC), one of the last bastions of tradition, had to bow before the winds of modernity by constructing a new media centre at the Nursery End of the Lord's ground. Named Spaceship, it was built at a cost of £5.8 million (\$ 9.3 million), and can accomodate 250 journalists and broadcasters. It was unveiled on 27 April 1999, seventeen days before the start of the World Cup.

There was now a permanent ICC World Cup Trophy crafted in silver and gilt in London by Garrard, the Crown jewellers, featuring a golden globe held aloft by three silver columns. Valued at more than £27,000, it is 60 centimetres in height and weighs 11 kilograms. The golden globe is presented in the form of a stylised cricket ball. The silver columns, which are designed as stumps and bails, represent the three pillars of cricket - batting, bowling and fielding. Australia had the honour of winning it.

This time the title sponsorship was not awarded. Instead there were four global partners - Emirates Airlines, NatWest Bank, Pepsi and Vodafone. The tournament was christened ICC World Cup.

A total of £11 million was raised from sponsorship. Income from television grossed £23 million from a global audience of 2.3 billion in 129 countries. There was a record profit of more than £30 million from this World Cup. The English Cricket Board (ECB) kept all the gate receipts and merchandising revenue, while the money received from award of television rights and sponsorship was divided between the participants. The ECB thus raked in £13.7 million, while the other Test playing nations received £1.425 million each, except Bangladesh whose share was £225,000.

The prize money on offer was close to £600,000 ($1 million), with the winners receiving £180,000 and the runners-up taking home £90,000. The losing semi-finalists received £60,000 each. The rest of the prize money, amounting to around £210,000 was shared by the other eight participants. A Daewoo Musso car, prize for the player-of-the-tournament, was won by the dashing South African allrounder Lance Klusener.

Bangladesh, who won the ICC Trophy 1997, and runners-up Kenya had already gained One-day International status. For the former it was the first appearance in the World Cup, as it was for Scotland who finished third in the tournament for the associate member countries. Group A comprised England, India, Kenya, South Africa, Sri Lanka and Zimbabwe, while in Group B were Australia, Bangladesh, New Zealand, Pakistan, Scotland and the West Indies.

The Cricket World Cup

For the first time there was a super-six stage. This was an improvement on the previous format wherein it was almost a foregone conclusion as to which eight teams would advance to the quarter-finals. This is not meant as disrespect towards Zimbabwe, but even in 1996 they were considered the weakest of the nine Test-playing nations. In the super-six, the three teams that qualified from Group A: South Africa, India and Zimbabwe, played each of the three qualifiers from Group B: Pakistan, Australia and New Zealand.

There were flaws in this system too. The points that teams carried forward from the group matches to the super-six were only those that they earned against the two teams that qualified from their group. Hence, Zimbabwe who finished third in Group A, carried 4 points, top team South Africa took with them 2 points, while second-placed India got none. Zimbabwe, who did not win a single super-six match, nearly made it to the semi-final. Eventual champions Australia, who won all three super-six matches, advanced to the semi-finals only by virtue of their victory in the last match against South Africa. There could easily have been a travesty of justice. The Duckworth-Lewis system of re-setting targets, which the average cricket enthusiast does not understand anyway, is another that might create a huge problem some day. In this, target scores can sometimes get enhanced, and a team that scores more can lose, in rain-interrupted matches. One-day cricket in general, and the World Cup in particular, could do with a simpler, more rational system.

About a year later, allegations of match-fixing took some sheen off this highly successful tournament. It cast a shadow over the game for a long time.

Pakistan beat New Zealand to enter the final. In the other semi-final there was a thrilling tie between Australia and South Africa, the first in the World Cup. Australia made it to the final as they had beaten South Africa in their earlier match. The Australians went on to emulate the West Indies by winning the World Cup for the second time.

The final:

Lord's, London, 20 June 1999

Australia won by 8 wickets

Pakistan: *132 all out in 39 overs (Shane Warne 4 for 33)*

Australia: *133 for 2 wickets in 20.1 overs (Mark Waugh 37 not out, Adam Gilchrist 54)*

Man of the Match: Shane Warne

Player of the Tournament: Lance Klusener

2003

The World Cup travelled to Africa for the first time in 2003. This was without doubt the biggest and best-organised tournament with fifty-two matches played in 15 grounds across South Africa, Zimbabwe and Kenya. Fourteen countries, the most ever assembled, paraded their talent. Namibia made their maiden appearance, having finished runners-up in the ICC Trophy for associate members. Canada staged a comeback after 24 years, while ICC Trophy winners Holland reappeared after missing the previous event. Never before had all six continents inhabited by man been represented at the same World Cup.

Global Cricket Corporation bagged the sponsorship rights for ICC tournaments, including the 2003 and 2007 World Cups, for $550 million. LG Electronics and Pepsi reportedly committed $30 million each to Global Cricket Corporation for the status of global partners for the 2003 and 2007 World Cups. The official sponsors of the 2003 World Cup were Hero Honda and South African Airways. The official regional sponsors were Hutchison/Orange, MTN, South African Breweries, Standard Bank and Vodafone, while Toyota were the official suppliers.

In a tournament that sprung many surprises, Australia remained unconquered, pulling off a string of eleven victories. They rivalled the feat of the West Indies by lifting the Cup for the second consecutive time and, in fact, surpassed Clive Lloyd's mighty team, claiming their third title overall. This was also

Australia's third successive final, a clear indication that they were far ahead of other teams in contemporary cricket.

The mascot was, appropriately, Dazzler the zebra, signifying the integration of the blacks and whites. Dazzler in various cricketing poses was one of the enduring images of this tournament. The logo too comprised zebra stripes with a patch of yellow.

The prize money on offer this time multiplied five-fold to $5 million. The champions took home a bonanza of $2 million. The runners-up received $800,000, and the losing semi-finalists $400,000 each. At last, the players who make it all happen, got due reward for their toil. A Golden Bat was instituted for the player-of-the-tournament. It was won by a batsman ranked among the all-time greats, India's Sachin Tendulkar, and presented appropriately by the incomparable Sir Garfield Sobers.

If cricket made its peace with the modern world in 1992, it merged completely with the ethos of the twenty-first century in 2003. The opening ceremony, inspired by that of the Sydney Olympics 2000, reflected the transition that the game had made. It was a spectacular display at Cape Town, the ethnic blending splendidly with the contemporary and showcasing the African way of life. It was at once dazzling, vibrant and colourful, and so infectious that the performers and the crowd rocked in unison. It was not just about cricket, it was about life itself, about the joy of living, about the thrill of making a collective surge towards prosperity. Several million dollars were spent on it. About 5000 volunteers took part, many from the under-privileged sections of society who were made to feel that they too matter. An estimated 1.2 billion people saw it on television.

The tournament was brilliantly organised. Careful thought was given to every aspect. Security fears were allayed. The wickets were, for the most part, ideal for One-day cricket and fair to both batsmen and bowlers. Special equipment was used to monitor the amount of bounce. There was some lateral movement, but not too much. The best batsmen got the opportunity to give full vent to their skills, and the best bowlers just rewards for their toil. The numerous sterling performances were a direct consequence of the quality of wickets and perhaps also an indication of how rapidly the game has changed. This was reflected in the several rapid-fire innings that were played, and the fact that pacemen seemed to be attacking instead of being restrictive. There was serious introspection about playing conditions. Night matches were held only at Cape Town and Durban. It was felt that at that time of the year there would be too much dew at the other centres, and that might unduly affect the result of matches. It is this attention to detail that makes an event memorable. A feature of the tournament was that officials kept away from the spotlight. They made a fleeting, dignified appearance at the opening ceremony and then briefly at the end. The man-of-the-match awards were presented by great cricketers from around the world and also top African sportspersons, who were designated ambassadors of the tournament.

A special mention must be made of Dr. Ali Bacher, executive

director of the tournament. He took up the post two years prior to the event and turned it into an unprecedented success. Captain of the brilliant South African Test team of 1970 just before they were banished from international cricket, Bacher kept the game alive in South Africa during the years of exile by organising rebel tours from Australia, England, West Indies and Sri Lanka. When South Africa were welcomed back to the fold in 1991, he guided the team close to the top as executive head of the United Cricket Board of South Africa. The 2003 World Cup is yet another feather in the cap of this outstanding administrator.

The total attendance was 626,845 people, which was 76 percent of the total capacity. The final at Johannesburg broke the record for South African grounds with a crowd of 32,827.

Yet for several months leading up to the tournament it was not cricket, but peripheral issues that made the headlines. Even prior to the ICC Champions Trophy 2002 there was wrangling about the terms of contracts offered to players, particularly clauses relating to ambush marketing. Indian players, in the main, objected as the terms interfered with their personal endorsements. Matters reached a head as the World Cup drew near, but ultimately an uneasy truce prevailed and the best players participated. The sooner the ICC, various boards, players and sponsors resolve this irksome problem the better it shall be for the game.

Politics was once again an unwelcome intruder. For a long time and up to the last minute England threatened to withdraw from their fixture in Zimbabwe due to the political situation there and fears over security of their players. Ultimately they forfeited the match, which contributed to their early exit from the tournament. New Zealand paid a similar price at a later stage for withdrawing from their game in Kenya, also due to security concerns.

Away from these aberrations, it was One-day cricket of a very high order. For some reason, though, there were not many close matches. Defending champions Australia were drawn in pool A along with England, Holland, India, Namibia, Pakistan and Zimbabwe. Pool B comprised Bangladesh, Canada, Kenya, New Zealand, South Africa, Sri Lanka and the West Indies. Australia, India and Zimbabwe advanced to the super-six where they met Sri Lanka, Kenya and New Zealand. This time one point was carried over by these teams for their wins over each of the teams that did not advance to the super-six, in addition to the four points earned for victories over sides that made it beyond the first stage. It was a more equitable system compared to the one in 1999, but still needed improvement to ensure that one upset did not result in the better teams failing to advance to the semi-finals.

The Duckworth-Lewis method was again the subject of much debate. This time hosts South Africa were at the centre of it. As rain intervened they made a dash for what they thought was the winning target against Sri Lanka. To their horror they found themselves a run short, and the tie ensured that they were bundled out in the first stage itself. That took some of the sheen off this splendid tournament. The ICC has to closely re-examine the Duckworth-Lewis method. There is no doubt that a simpler formula must be evolved, one that is easily understood and does not require constant reference to charts. Cricket must be played with willow and leather, not log tables.

The Kenyans were a revelation. They shocked Sri Lanka on home turf by dint of some inspired performances and marched into the super-six. A victory over Zimbabwe earned them a semi-final spot against India. Their success was a shot-in-the-arm for cricket in Kenya and wonderful for the game itself. It also resulted in their securing sponsorship, which they had long sought in vain. Australia advanced relentlessly and came up against Sri Lanka in the penultimate stage. The final was between the two best teams in the event, but the Australians packed far too many guns for India who had surpassed expectations after making a tentative start in the tournament.

The final:

New Wanderers Stadium, Johannesburg, 23 March 2003

Australia won by 125 runs

Australia: *359 for 2 wickets in 50 overs (Adam Gilchrist 57, Matthew Hayden 37, Ricky Ponting 140 not out, Damien Martyn 88 not out)*

India: *234 all out in 39.2 overs (Virender Sehwag 82, Rahul Dravid 47, Glenn McGrath 3 for 52)*

Man of the Match: Ricky Ponting

Player of the Tournament: Sachin Tendulkar

2007

The World Cup came a full circle in 2007 when the West Indies had the honour of staging it. It should have been a watershed for West Indies cricket, which languished in the nineties after the magnificent Lloyd-Richards era of the seventies and eighties, and indeed the earlier glorious days of Constantine, Headley, the three Ws - Worrell, Weekes and Walcott, and the peerless Sobers. Not only did the supply line of world-class players dry up either side of the turn of the century, West Indies cricket in general went into decline. There seemed to be complacency, financial constraints were a bane, pitches turned into lifeless sandpits and the team depended on the performances of three or four stars. Not surprisingly, West Indies failed to reach a World Cup final after 1983, coming close to it only in 1996. The dreadful slump must have hurt.

But there were clear signs of a turnaround. With a streamlined administration, Brian Lara regaining his magical touch, a batting line-up at par with the best in the world, promising young bowlers beginning to emerge and wickets showing signs of life, West Indies cricket appeared to be on the high road towards re-scaling the pinnacles of yore. It would have been a fair reward for the most enthusiastic and joyous crowd in world cricket. Through the days of ignominy, it had been the delightful crowds at the West Indies grounds that kept their cricket going. They deserved a feast and were dearly wishing that their team would provide the dessert. Lara would certainly have been yearning for a triumphant theme to his swansong, a high note in the evening of a glittering career.

In the words of the ICC, the logo of the 2007 World Cup "expresses the joy and exuberance of cricketers and cricket fans worldwide, in a Caribbean setting. The vibrant red figure central to the logo captures the exuberant energy of dance and celebration. The colour red represents the passion that the fans both in the West Indies and the world have for the game of cricket. The positioning of the bat and ball are figurative elements of the palm tree forming the trunk and fruit. The vibrant green of the crown of the palm tree, and the azure blue which stands for the surrounding sky and seas are the backdrop in which the prestigious tournament will take place."

The mascot of the 2007 World Cup was a teenage character called 'Mello', who embodied the lifestyle of the region, 'cheeky and curious and socially aware like so many young people today.'

Hero Honda and Hutch joined LG Electronics and Pepsi as global partners of the ICC. The telecommunications behemoth, Cable & Wireless, long associated with West Indies cricket, was the principal telecom provider to the event, and an official sponsor alongside Indian Oil and Scotiabank.

The prize money remained static at $5 million, but the teams took home larger amounts. The champions were awarded $2.24 million, while the runners-up received $1 million. The losing semi-finalists got $45,000 each, while the teams that finished

The Cricket World Cup

fifth to eighth were awarded $200,000, $150,000, $100,000 and $50,000 respectively. In the group matches, the winning teams took away $10,000 and the losing teams a consolation of $5,000. The player of the tournament prize was a diamond studded cricket ball crafted at Kolkata, worth Rs. 30,00,000 ($ 60,000), won appropriately by Glenn McGrath.

The ICC's Venue Assessment Team, using the most stringent standards, chose eight venues: Antigua & Barbuda, Barbados, Grenada, Guyana, Jamaica I, St. Kitts & Nevis, St. Lucia, and Trinidad & Tobago. Capacity in all the grounds, except St. Kitts, was enhanced to seat at least 20,000 spectators. Jamaica, headquarters of the ICC World Cup 2007 Inc., had the privilege of staging the opening ceremony and opening match, as well as the first semi-final. All preliminary round matches in Group D were played here at the Sabina Park in the capital city, Kingston. The second semi-final was held in St. Lucia at the state-of-the-art Beausejour Stadium in the resort town of Gros Islet. The preliminary round matches in Group C were staged at this venue.

Kensington Oval, dubbed fondly as The Mecca by the locals, at Bridgetown, the capital of Barbados, was chosen to host the final, and also six super-eight matches. Home to the Pickwick Cricket Club since 1882, the ground has hosted international fixtures since 1895, including the first Test match played in the West Indies in 1930 against England. A new stadium came up here to hold 31,000 spectators, more than doubling its earlier capacity of 15,000.

Group A teams battled in out in the refurbished Warner Park at

Basseterre, the capital of St. Kitts & Nevis, where the capacity is just 10,000. The preliminary round matches of Group B were played at the Queen's Park Oval, Port of Spain in Trinidad & Tobago. Even though hitherto it had the largest seating capacity in the Caribbean, a new stadium was built here too, capable of holding 25,000 people.

The other three venues staged only super-eight games. The brand new Queen's Park Stadium at St. George's, the capital of Grenada, was one of these arenas. Sadly, the Antigua Recreation Ground, headquarters of the West Indies Cricket Board, and where Brian Lara twice broke the record for the highest Test score, did not see World Cup action as a result. The Antigua & Barbuda government ordered a new stadium named after the legendary Sir Vivian Richards, which was built at North Sound, outside its capital St. John's. Interestingly, China paid $23 million to construct this facility.

A new stadium was also built in Guyana at Providence, near the capital Georgetown to replace the Bourda Oval. The Government of India provided assistance, the cost of $25 million being met through a $6 million grant and an Exim Bank loan on concessional terms.

Bermuda, Jamaica II, St. Vincent & Grenadines, and the United States of America were the four venues that lost out. There was much talk about staging four matches in the United States, one of which would have been in Disney World, Florida. Though the United States finished sixth and last in the ICC Trophy 2005, they would have gained automatic entry as co-hosts of the 2007 World Cup. That would have given tremendous fillip to the game in that country. America has a longer history of cricket than is generally believed. The game was introduced there in the early 18th century by the British, and John Adams, one of the founding fathers of the nation, was also one of its first cricketers. The first-ever international cricket match was held between the United States and Canada in 1844 at the St. George's Cricket Club Ground in Bloomingdale Park, New York. The US team beat the West Indies on January 5, 1888, and more recently won the American Championships in 2002, during which they beat Canada by three wickets. There are 10,000 players representing 500 clubs in 29 leagues across New York, California - which has four turf wickets - Florida, Chicago, Texas and New Jersey. Ultimately the strict security measures that would have been enforced for entry into the United States, following the 9/11 attacks, deterred the ICC from staging matches there. Cricket will have to wait awhile before it gains a foothold in the richest market in the world.

The eleven teams with One-day International status were seeded according to their rankings in the ICC table as on 1 April 2005. Five other qualifiers came in, based on their performances in the ICC Trophy held in Ireland in July 2005. The winners of that tournament, Scotland, and fifth-placed Holland joined Australia and South Africa in Group A. Bermuda, fourth in the ICC Trophy, were put alongside Sri Lanka, India and Bangladesh in Group B. The third qualifiers Canada were placed with New Zealand, England and Kenya in Group C, while runners-up Ireland found themselves in Group D along with Pakistan, West Indies and Zimbabwe. The ICC spent up to $500,000 on each of the five qualifiers to prepare for the World Cup and development of cricket in these associate member countries. The groups and seedings were as under:

Group A at St. Kitts : Australia (1), South Africa (5), Scotland (12), Holland (16).

Group B at Trinidad : Sri Lanka (2), India (8), Bangladesh (11), Bermuda (15).

Group C at St. Lucia : New Zealand (3), England (7), Kenya (10), Canada (14).

Group D at Jamaica : Pakistan (4), West Indies (6), Zimbabwe (9), Ireland (13).

There were exciting possibilities. Despite setbacks like the players' endorsements controversy, the tournament was believed to be the turbo that West Indies cricket needed to re-charge itself. The event was televised in 200 countries to an estimated viewership of two billion. The World Cup had come a long way since that day in 1975 when all the top cricketers of the world assembled at Buckingham Palace to meet the Queen. One could almost see the calypso kings swaying in anticipation.

What actually happened was not only stunning and entirely unexpected but turned this into the most tragic World Cup of all. First the brand new stadiums with every modern facility at hand, but many located miles out of the way were too inaccessible for the local populace. Their very character was so distinct from the homely Caribbean party venues that the old stadiums were. To make matters worse the high ticket prices were a huge deterrent to the average West Indian fan, along with stifling security that prohibited them from bringing in not only their own food and placards but also musical instruments that are an integral part of joyous Caribbean cricket. It was avaricious and officious administration at its worst, and it came as no surprise that the officials were roundly booed at the closing ceremony. There were sparse crowds at all the grounds. They reached a nadir at the Warner Park, Basseterre, St. Kitts where less than 1,500 people saw Herschelle Gibbs hit 6 sixes in an over. Only in five of the 24 group matches did the crowd exceed 10,000, the highest being in the opening clash between the hosts and Pakistan at Sabina Park in Kingston, and the India-Sri Lanka encounter at Queens Park Oval, Port of Spain, when the figure exceeded 16,000. The average attendance in the group matches was less than 7,000.

There was an improvement from the super-eight stage onwards, and even though restrictions were eased, there was never a capacity crowd. The largest assembly was at Brian Lara's farewell game, the last super-eight face-off with England at the famous Kensington Oval at Bridgetown, when 22,452 fans arrived. The next highest was in the final, the official attendance figure being 20,108, again at Kensington Oval, which has a capacity of 31,000. The average attendance figure through the super-eight to the final was just over 10,000. Still, the gate receipts were double that of the previous World Cup at $32 million. The moot point was whether the same, or better, result could have been achieved with lower ticket prices but much larger crowds.

The format of the tournament was changed, bringing in two more teams, making a total of 16 participants. There were, therefore, four groups of four teams each, with the top two in each group advancing to a super-eight league. This brought its own set of problems. There were far too many matches against and between the weaker sides. Of the 24 group matches, there were obviously only four games, one in each group, contested between the top eight teams. One upset was likely to topple the applecart, which it did in two groups and sent India and Pakistan crashing out of the tournament after playing only three matches each. This not only took away huge numbers of television viewers but also necessitated half the 24 super-eight matches involving unfancied outfits like Bangladesh and first-timers Ireland.

The shock defeat of Pakistan at the hands of Ireland also had a horrible fallout. The next morning their coach Bob Woolmer was found dead in his hotel bathroom. Then followed one of the most bizarre and sorrowful episodes in the history of sport. All kinds of conjectures and insinuations flew about. Crack sleuths were brought in, inquests were held, there were murder theories, stories about the betting mafia and deranged fans did the rounds, the needle of suspicion was even pointed at the players. The whole tournament was vitiated, and the sordid saga dragged on for months after. Ultimately it was concluded that the genial man had died of natural causes. In all probability, stress got the better of him; the intense scrutiny and censure must have been too much to endure.

There was a lot of splendid cricket played during the tournament but Woolmer's death cast a dark shadow over everything else. Australia marched on relentlessly. Such was their dominance that they never lost more than six wickets in a match, and a couple of their tailenders did not get a chance to bat at all. On the other hand, they bowled out their opponents every time except in two matches, in one of which they prised out six wickets in a 22-over innings, and in the other captured eight wickets in the 36-over Sri Lankan knock in the final. It was awesome cricket. Australia were not clear favourites this time, but they won all their matches for the second World Cup in a row, wresting their third successive title, and appearing in their fourth consecutive final. By doing so, they surpassed Clive Lloyd's great West Indies side and set near-impossible benchmarks for other teams to emulate.

Just as everyone was heaving a sigh of relief when the rain-interrupted, truncated final was drawing to a close, the light was offered to the Sri Lankan batsmen after 33 overs, and everyone trudged off. The Australians had begun to celebrate and preparations for the presentation had started. But hullo, what's this? The umpires Aleem Dar and Steve Bucknor decreed that the match was not over and that everyone would need to come back on the morrow to complete the remaining three overs, even though the minimum 20 overs had been bowled. It was amazing that neither the match referee Jeff Crowe nor the reserve umpires Rudi Koertzen and Billy Bowden prevailed on the on-field umpires to end a match that was already over. Ultimately it took a gentlemen's agreement between the two captains Ricky Ponting and Mahela Jayawardene to end the impasse. The Sri

Lankan skipper sent out his batsmen in near darkness and the Australian chief put on his slow bowlers to conclude the farce. Never before had the final of a sporting event of this magnitude ended in such embarrassing circumstances. That the five match officials were suspended for the next ICC event, the Twenty20 World Championship later that year, was hardly of concern to billions of disgusted fans around the world.

It might be uncharitable, but quite often the word used for this tournament was 'fiasco', even though there were lots of stirring deeds with bat and ball. Indeed, off-field events overtook the exciting action in the brand new stadiums of the exotic Caribbean islands. Not since the 1972 Olympics at Munich had a sadder sporting international event been staged. It was time for cricket to make a new beginning.

The final:

Kensington Oval, Bridgetown, Barbados, 28 April 2007

Australia won by 53 runs (D/L method)

Australia: *281 for 4 wickets in 38 overs (Adam Gilchrist 149, Matthew Hayden 38, Ricky Ponting 37)*

Sri Lanka: *215 for 8 wickets in 36 overs (Sanath Jayasuriya 63, Kumar Sangakkara 54)*

Man of the Match : Adam Gilchrist

Player of the Tournament : Glenn McGrath

2011

The World Cup comes back to the sub-continent for the third time in 2011. On this occasion it will be staged in India, Sri Lanka and Bangladesh. There are now 14 teams in the fray, two less than in 2007. The ten full members get direct entry, including Zimbabwe, even though they are at present suspended from Test matches. In the qualifying tournament held in South Africa for associate members in 2009, Ireland beat Canada by nine wickets in the final at Centurion. These two countries will be joined by Holland and Kenya on the big stage.

The super-league has been done away with, and the teams will advance from the group matches to the quarter-finals. It is akin to the format of the 1996 World Cup, also played in the sub-continent, but with two more teams now. In this manner there will be 49 matches instead of the 51 played in 2007, and the event will be about a week shorter. The groups are as follows:

Group A : Australia, Pakistan, New Zealand, Sri Lanka, Zimbabwe, Canada and Kenya.

Group B : India, South Africa, England, West Indies, Bangladesh, Ireland and Holland.

The opening ceremony and first match between co-hosts Bangladesh and India will be held at the Sher-e-Bangla National Stadium in Mirpur, on the outskirts of the capital Dhaka. Two new stadiums are coming up in Sri Lanka. The Pallekele International Cricket Stadium, being constructed at a cost of $4 million at Kandy, will hold 35,000 spectators, while the Suriyawewa Stadium at Hambantota on the south-eastern coast, dotted with tourist resorts, will have a seating capacity of 33,000, a project costing about $8 million. The capacity of Colombo's Premadasa Stadium was increased from 12,000 to 30,000. Bangladesh will play all their six group matches at home in Dhaka and Chittagong, while India will play the rest of their matches on their own soil. Eight venues have been chosen in India - Ahmedabad, Bangalore, Chennai, Kolkata, Mohali, Mumbai, Nagpur and New Delhi. Sri Lanka, like India, will be seen in action on home territory, except for their last league match which will be staged in Mumbai.

Owing to security concerns, the 14 matches scheduled to be held in Pakistan have been relocated, and their team will be based in Sri Lanka. Not only all of Pakistan's league matches but their quarter-final and semi-final too - should they reach those stages - will be held in Sri Lanka at the Premadasa Stadium in Colombo. The other semi-final will be staged at the Punjab Cricket Association Stadium in Mohali. The final will be held at the Wankhede Stadium, which is being renovated. India will host 29 matches, while Sri Lanka and Bangladesh will stage 12 and 8 games respectively.

An elephant, christened Stumpy, has been chosen as the mascot of the 2011 World Cup. According to the organizing committee, "The idea of our mascot is to crystallise the feelings and action of the sport and the fans in a graphic form that reflects the visceral tone and emotion that cricket creates in its followers, especially in an event like the cricket World Cup. It

The Cricket World Cup

also emphasises the enthusiasm of youth both in general and for cricket itself, especially on the sub-continent with its massive and dedicated following. He's stylised to give an instantly recognisable graphic strength so that with exposure his bold lines and strong colouring will instantly create a friendly face for the cricket World Cup."

The total prize money has been doubled to $10 million, of which the champions will carry away $4 million. The television rights have been secured by ESPN Star Sports for $2 billion, with the event being telecast live in 220 countries.

THE SCHEDULE

Thursday 17 February	Opening Ceremony	Dhaka

Group Matches

Saturday 19 February	Bangladesh v India	Dhaka
Sunday 20 February	Kenya v New Zealand	Chennai
Sunday 20 February	Canada v Sri Lanka	Hambantota
Monday 21 February	Australia v Zimbabwe	Ahmedabad
Tuesday 22 February	England v Holland	Nagpur
Wednesday 23 February	Kenya v Pakistan	Hambantota
Thursday 24 February	South Africa v West Indies	New Delhi
Friday 25 February	Australia v New Zealand	Nagpur
Friday 25 February	Bangladesh v Ireland	Dhaka
Saturday 26 February	Pakistan v Sri Lanka	Colombo
Sunday 27 February	England v India	Kolkata
Monday 28 February	Holland v West Indies	New Delhi
Monday 28 February	Canada v Zimbabwe	Nagpur
Tuesday 1 March	Kenya v Sri Lanka	Colombo
Wednesday 2 March	England v Ireland	Bangalore
Thursday 3 March	Holland v South Africa	Mohali
Thursday 3 March	Canada v Pakistan	Colombo
Friday 4 March	New Zealand v Zimbabwe	Ahmedabad
Friday 4 March	Bangladesh v West Indies	Dhaka

Saturday 5 March	Australia v Sri Lanka	Colombo
Sunday 6 March	India v Ireland	Bangalore
Sunday 6 March	England v South Africa	Chennai
Monday 7 March	Canada v Kenya	New Delhi
Tuesday 8 March	New Zealand v Pakistan	Pallekele
Wednesday 9 March	Holland v India	New Delhi
Thursday 10 March	Sri Lanka v Zimbabwe	Pallekelle
Friday 11 March	Bangladesh v England	Chittagong
Friday 11 March	Ireland v West Indies	Mohali
Saturday 12 March	India v South Africa	Nagpur
Sunday 13 March	Canada v New Zealand	Mumbai
Sunday 13 March	Australia v Kenya	Bangalore
Monday 14 March	Bangladesh v Holland	Chittagong
Monday 14 March	Pakistan v Zimbabwe	Pallekelle
Tuesday 15 March	Ireland v South Africa	Kolkata
Wednesday 16 March	Australia v Canada	Bangalore
Thursday 17 March	England v West Indies	Chennai
Friday 18 March	New Zealand v Sri Lanka	Mumbai
Friday 18 March	Holland v Ireland	Kolkata
Saturday 19 March	Bangladesh v South Africa	Dhaka
Saturday 19 March	Australia v Pakistan	Colombo
Sunday 20 March	Kenya v Zimbabwe	Kolkata
Sunday 20 March	India v West Indies	Chennai

Quarter-finals

Wednesday 23 March	First quarter-final	Dhaka
Thursday 24 March	Second quarter-final	Colombo
Friday 25 March	Third quarter-final	Dhaka
Saturday 26 March	Fourth quarter-final	Ahmedabad

Semi-finals

Tuesday 29 March	First semi-final	Colombo
Wednesday 30 March	Second semi-final	Mohali

Final

Saturday 2 April	Final	Mumbai

Thrilling Encounters

Thrilling Encounters

Last-wicket heroics

Pakistan v West Indies
Birmingham, June 11, 1975

Deryck Murray

The innate lazy elegance of Majid Khan, deputising for skipper Asif Iqbal, was in full evidence as he played a strokeful knock of 60. Mushtaq Mohammad drew on all his experience, and later Wasim Raja played some belligerent shots, both hitting half-centuries. Pakistan set a challenging target of 267 in 60 overs for the fancied West Indies. In a devastating burst, Sarfraz Nawaz had Gordon Greenidge and Alvin Kallicharran caught behind, and trapped Roy Fredericks leg-before. Sarfraz had taken three for 8 in 3.4 overs. Veteran Rohan Kanhai helped his captain Clive Lloyd stage a minor recovery. Then began a regular procession. At 166 for eight, an upset win for Pakistan seemed a certainty. Deryck Murray dug in his heels. He put on 37 runs for the ninth wicket with Vanburn Holder. The wily Sarfraz returned to have Holder snapped up. From 203 for nine, Murray and Andy Roberts inched towards their target. Amid mounting tension the West Indies pulled off a sensational win with two balls to spare.

Pakistan 266 for 7 wickets (60 overs)
West Indies 267 for 9 wickets (59.4 overs)

Bumper barrage

Australia v Sri Lanka
Kennington Oval, London, June 11, 1975

Jeff Thomson

Sri Lanka were the minnows. Still years away from attaining Test status, they were expected to offer token resistance. They had crashed to an ignominious 86 all out against the West Indies. Now Aussies Alan Turner and Rick McCosker put on 182. Turner raced to a century. Greg Chappell and Doug Walters featured in a 117-run stand. A target of 329 seemed beyond the Lankans. But there was drama. Ranjit Fernando began with four boundaries. Bandula Warnapura helped Sunil Wettimuny put on 54. Soon sparks began to fly. Dennis Lillee and Jeff Thomson were never charitable towards batsmen. Now their pride was hurt by this insolence. Wettimuny and Duleep Mendis sailed along. At 150 for two, Thomson pitched one short which felled Mendis. Wettimuny was hit twice in the ribs, then on the foot. The intrepid Lankans would not throw in the towel. Michael Tissera joined Anura Tennekoon. At 246, only two wickets had fallen. Ian Chappell struck twice with his part-time leg-spin. The Lankans fell short by 52 runs. They took the physical battering but the Aussies got a rude shake up.

Australia 328 for 5 wickets (60 overs)
Sri Lanka 276 for 4 wickets (60 overs)

A clinical approach

India v New Zealand
Manchester, June 14, 1975

Glenn Turner

India made a poor start as six wickets fell for 101 to a versatile New Zealand attack. The perky allrounder Abid Ali scored a splendid 70 and India were able reach a respectable total of 230. New Zealand had a classy batsman in their captain Glenn Turner, then at the height of his powers. Ranged against him was Bishan Singh Bedi, one of the greatest left-arm spinners ever. Conceding only 28 runs off his twelve overs, half of which were scoreless, Bedi had Turner's opening partner John Morrison caught behind. As wickets fell regularly at the other end, Turner stood firm. The overs began to run out, and the asking-rate hovered around six per over. Turner took charge. His long years with Worcestershire stood him in good stead as he steered his team towards the target. The Indian attack toiled in vain. There were only seven deliveries remaining when New Zealand rode home. Glenn Turner with his brilliant unbeaten 114 was the difference between the two sides. India were indeed still learning the ropes.

India 230 all out (60 overs)
New Zealand 233 for 6 wickets (58.5 overs)

Swinging with the wind

Australia v England (semi-final)
Leeds, June 18, 1975

Gary Gilmour

It was reckoned that Gary Gilmour would emulate the feats of the great left-handed Australian allrounder Alan Davidson - if not another Gary - Sobers. This match showed why Gilmour was rated so high. The conditions were just right for this left-arm paceman. Gilmour had England in deep trouble on the green-top from the very start. Dennis Amiss was leg-before to a wicked in-swinger, as were Keith Fletcher and Allan Knott, as also Frank Hayes who shouldered arms thinking the ball was leaving him. Another incoming delivery knocked out Barry Wood's off-stump. Tony Grieg was the only Gilmour victim claimed by a ball moving away. At the end of Gilmour's 12-over spell England were in disarray. He had taken all the six wickets for 14 runs, six of the overs being scoreless. It was the first time a bowler had taken six wickets in a One-day International, a truly devastating stint. England capsized for 93 off 36.2 overs. But they hit back in just as telling a fashion. At 39 for six the game could go either way. Doug Walters and Gilmour fought through the crisis to knock off the runs.

England 93 all out (36.2 overs)
Australia 94 for six wickets (28.4 overs)

Magnificent spectacle

Australia v West Indies (final)
Lord's, London, June 21, 1975

Clive Lloyd

The stage was set for a battle royale at the Mecca of cricket. Dennis Lillee bowled a well-directed bouncer and Roy Fredericks hooked it perfectly for a six. But Fredericks began to walk back to the pavilion, having dislodged the bails while completing the stroke. It was a dramatic start. The Australians bagged two more wickets. Skipper Clive Lloyd then belted the attack. The experienced Rohan Kanhai played an admirable foil. They put on a record 149 runs for the fourth wicket, the last 81 coming in just 9 overs. Lloyd hit up 102. Gary Gilmour picked up five wickets. The Aussies battled, but four brilliant run outs, all but one by Vivian Richards, set them back. At 233 for nine the Prudential Cup seemed to have found its first abode. The unlikely pair of Jeff Thomson and Dennis Lillee got together to try and carve out an even unlikelier win. Forty-one priceless runs had been added when Thomson rushed out of his crease. His desperate dive back was not enough as Deryck Murray effected a fifth run out, a thrilling finish to a great final.

West Indies 291 for 8 wickets (60 overs)
Australia 274 all out (58.4 overs)

Rock 'n roll

England v Pakistan
Leeds, June 16, 1979

Mike Hendrick

Skipper Mike Brearley was caught behind second ball off Imran Khan; so was Derek Randall off Sikander Bakht soon. After a brief respite, wickets fell regularly. At 118 for eight England appeared doomed. Wicketkeeper Bob Taylor and Bob Willis, hardly known for his prowess with the willow, battled it out. The Bobs put on 43 runs, which proved crucial in the ultimate analysis. Still, a score of 165 in 60 overs could not have inspired much confidence. Pakistan's comfortable start provided no hint of the turmoil to follow. In a devastating burst of eight deliveries, Mike Hendrick left the Pakistan innings in tatters. He removed Majid Khan, Mudassar Nazar, Sadiq Mohammed and Haroon Rashid. Ian Botham soon dismissed Javed Miandad and Zaheer Abbas. Pakistan were 34 for six. Asif Iqbal and Wasim Raja added 52. Imran Khan helped Asif put on 29 runs. Asif departed for 51. Imran and Wasim Bari added another 30. In desperation Brearley turned to Geoff Boycott's innocuous round-armers. He had Bari and Sikander Bakht caught. Pakistan fell short by 14 runs with four overs still to be bowled.

England 165 for 9 wickets (60 overs)
Pakistan 151 all out (56 overs)

Day of the minnows

Duleep Mendis

India v Sri Lanka
Manchester, June 16 & 18, 1979

Sri Lanka were only associate members of the ICC - then known as International Cricket Conference - while India were one of the major cricketing nations. Sri Lanka, though, had distinguished themselves often by their gritty performances in their limited appearances in the international arena. India, on the other hand, had shown remarkable naivete in the Limited-overs game on a number of occasions. A stunning upset could not be ruled as the sub-continental neighbours took the field at Old Trafford in this rain-marred match. Sunil Wettimuny and Roy Dias put on 96 runs for the second wicket. Duleep Mendis consolidated the position with a superb 64 with 3 huge sixes. The Indian progress was slow. They scored only 117 off 35 overs. Leg-spinner Somachandra de Silva destroyed the middle order. Five crucial wickets fell for only 43 runs. Medium-pacer Tony Opatha mopped up the tail. It was a great triumph for Sri Lanka by 47 runs with almost six overs to spare. This was the first time a Test-playing nation had been humbled in the World Cup by an associate member.

Sri Lanka 238 for 5 wickets (60 overs)
India 191 all out (54.1 overs)

Home advantage

England v New Zealand (semi-final)
Manchester, June 20, 1979

John Wright

Mike Brearley dug in, and added 58 runs with Graham Gooch for the third wicket. When Brearley was dismissed, 35 overs had gone and the score read 96 for three. Gooch kept firing till he was out for 71. The score then was 177 after 50 overs. Derek Randall, batting unusually low at no. 7, played a valuable hand in raising the run-rate. The last three overs produced 25 runs, taking the total to 221 for eight. John Wright and Bruce Edgar raised 47 for the first wicket. Glenn Turner played a determined innings but after 35 overs the score of 96 was the same as England's at that stage. After 50 overs, New Zealand had fallen behind, notching up only 154 runs. The asking-rate had climbed to nearly 7-per-over. Warren Lees, aided by Richard Hadlee and Lance Cairns, put up a brave fight. They were impeded by another fine display of seam bowling by Mike Hendrick. After 58 overs the score stood at 202 for eight. Hendrick shattered Lees' stumps in the crucial 59th over. Fourteen runs were needed in the last over. The Kiwis could not get Ian Botham away. England were home by 9 runs.

England 221 for 8 wickets (60 overs)
New Zealand 212 for 9 wickets (60 overs)

Champagne batting

Zaheer Abbas

Pakistan v West Indies (semi-final)
Kennington Oval, London, June 20, 1979

This match showed why the West Indies were the unchallenged kings of cricket at the time. It also revived memories of the thrilling contest between the two teams in the first World Cup. Gordon Greenidge and Desmond Haynes seized the initiative with a terrific assault, raising the 100 off 22.2 overs. Asif Iqbal had the rampaging Greenidge caught behind for 73 in a stand of 132. Vivian Richards was in no mood to relent He teamed up with Clive Lloyd to hand out a lashing. By the time they left, the score was 236 for four. Asif Iqbal had taken all the wickets while Majid Khan bowled a very tight spell. Collis King played some characteristically belligerent strokes. West Indies finished at 293 for six. Majid and Zaheer Abbas put the fearsome bowling to the sword. They added 166. Another 118 remained off 20 overs. Colin Croft dismissed the brilliant Zaheer. He had Majid and Javed Miandad too. Pakistan slumped from 176 for one in 40 overs, to 250 all out in 56.2 overs. But they showed that they could embarrass the best.

West Indies 293 for 6 wickets (60 overs)
Pakistan 250 all out (56.2 overs)

Ecstatic debut

Australia v Zimbabwe
Nottingham, June 9, 1983

Duncan Fletcher

Zimbabwe were the minnows. Put in against an accomplished Australian attack, Ali Shah and Grant Paterson raised 55 for the first wicket in 19 overs. The peerless Dennis Lillee removed both off successive deliveries. Soon at 94 for five the Zimbabwe innings seemed to have come apart. Duncan Fletcher, playing a captain's innings of 69 not out, ensured that it did not. He put on 70 for the sixth wicket with Kevin Curran. Finally Iain Butchart helped Fletcher add 75 runs, then a World Cup record for the seventh wicket. Aussies Graeme Wood and Kepler Wessels put on 61 runs before Fletcher made his presence felt again. He had Wood taken behind and without further ado, consumed his counterpart Kim Hughes. Fletcher claimed the first four wickets. Fifty-three runs were required off the last five overs with three wickets left. Rodney Marsh and Rodney Hogg went for the bowling. Still there were 23 runs needed in the last over. They managed only nine as Marsh hit a six and reached his half-century. Zimbabwe pulled off a stunning upset which set the trend for the tournament.

Zimbabwe 239 for 6 wickets (60 overs)
Australia 226 for 7 wickets (60 overs)

A jolt for the champs

Yash Pal Sharma

India v West Indies
Manchester, June 9 & 10, 1983

Twice-champions West Indies had never lost a World Cup match. That meant nine wins and one wash-out. India had won only one of their six matches - against non-descript East Africa eight years earlier - and finished last in their group in 1979. Only a brave man or a lunatic could predict anything other than a facile win for the West Indies. Expectedly, India were in trouble. Sandeep Patil played his typically belligerent strokes. Cheeky and gritty, Yashpal Sharma hit 89, perhaps the innings of his life. He put on 73 with Roger Binny. A total of 262 could stretch the champions. Gordon Greenidge and Desmond Haynes fell after a customary rousing start. With rain around, stumps were drawn at 67 for two off 22 overs. Vivian Richards was taken behind early off Binny. Wickets tumbled. At 157 for nine, the champions were in dire straits. Andy Roberts and Joel Garner raised 71 runs. The Indians kept their heads. Ravi Shastri enticed Garner, and Syed Kirmani removed the bails. The West Indies fell short by 34 runs. Almost six overs remained. It was another shocking result in this exciting World Cup.

India 262 for 8 wickets (60 overs)
West Indies 228 all out (54.1 overs)

Stirring fightback

England v New Zealand
Birmingham, June 15, 1983

Jeremy Coney

Graeme Fowler and Chris Tavare got England off to a comfortable start. Then the innings started to fall away. Only David Gower, continuing his good form, stood firm among the ruins. Grace and fluidity, ever the hallmarks of his batting, were in full evidence as he stroked a brilliant unbeaten 92 off just 96 balls. Richard Hadlee and Ewan Chatfield demolished the tail. England slumped to 234 all out. Bob Willis removed openers Glenn Turner and Bruce Edgar with only three runs scored. Geoff Howarth and Jeremy Coney added 71 for the fifth wicket. A lightning return from Graham Dilley ran out Howarth. The pendulum swung again. New Zealand hung on precariously at 151 for six. Richard Hadlee helped Coney realise 70 runs. In his last burst Willis bowled Hadlee, and trapped Lance Cairns leg-before. At 231 for eight Paul Allott bowled the final over. With two deliveries remaining the scores were level. Amid mounting tension, John Bracewell cracked the fifth ball to the boundary.

England 234 all out (55.2 overs)
New Zealand 238 for 8 wickets (59.5 overs)

A bridge too far

Pakistan v Sri Lanka
Leeds, June 16, 1983

Imran Khan

In an inspired spell, Asantha de Mel removed Mohsin Khan, Mansoor Akhtar and Zaheer Abbas. Rumesh Ratnayake had Javed Miandad and Ijaz Fakih leg-before at 43. Injury prevented skipper Imran Khan from bowling that summer, but the great allrounder shone with the bat. Joining him was rookie seamer Shahid Mahboob. Shahid went hell-bent-for-leather. In a way he was at home in Yorkshire, having played for Hartshead Moor in the Bradford league. They put on a record 144 runs. De Mel had Shahid caught, and removed Sarfraz Nawaz too. Imran hit a magnificent 102 not out. De Mel shared the honours with a splendid five for 39. Sidath Wettimuny and Roy Dias got up to hundred for only one wicket. Dias fell after a characteristic display of delightful shots. Not one to be shackled, Duleep Mendis attacked, but fell going for one big shot too many. Disaster struck in the shape of leg-spinning wizard, Abdul Qadir. Sri Lanka slumped to 199 for nine, now needing 37 off six overs. Pulses were racing as 25 runs came off 4.2 overs. A slower one from the wily Sarfraz had de Mel holing out to Imran. Pakistan won by 11 runs with 9 balls left.

Pakistan 235 for 7 wickets (60 overs)
Sri Lanka 224 all out (58.3 overs)

Thrilling Encounters

Indian rope trick

India v West Indies (final)
Lord's, London, June 25, 1983

Mohinder Amarnath

Lord's was bathed in sunshine, ready to crown the undisputed kings of cricket with another title. The conquerors from the Caribbean marshalled by elder statesman Clive Lloyd were poised for a hat-trick. Joel Garner's steeply rising deliveries bowled from his great height, were impossible to get away. Sunil Gavaskar fished at Andy Roberts to be taken by Jeff Dujon. Krish Srikkanth dazzled in customary fashion, including a hooked six off Roberts. Mohinder Amarnath and Yashpal Sharma consolidated. But disaster struck. Last pair Syed Kirmani and Balwinder Sandhu made the total look less pitiable at 183 off 54.4 overs. A sensational start saw Gordon Greenidge bowled for 1, shouldering arms to a Sandhu in-dipper. That set up a grand entry by the imperious Vivian Richards. He batted like the monarch he often was at the crease, smashing the ball around the hallowed ground. He skied Madan Lal. Kapil Dev turned and ran. It seemed an eternity before the Indian skipper clung on to the prize. The door opened for the underdogs. Soon it was 76 for six. It was a sensational upset when the day's hero Amarnath trapped Michael Holding leg-before.

India 183 all out (54.4 overs)
West Indies 140 all out (52 overs)

Chilling Thriller

Australia v India
Madras, October 9, 1987

Navjot Singh Sidhu

Amid great excitement the reigning champions appeared on home turf. For the visitors, David Boon and Geoff Marsh put on 110. The belligerent Dean Jones helped consolidate. Marsh notched up a century. A total of 270 in 50 overs had the home supporters worried. Sunil Gavaskar and Krish Srikkanth, gave a flying start. For once, Gavaskar outscored his unorthodox big-hitting partner. Next came Navjot Singh Sidhu, whose clean hitting had been a revelation. Srikkanth and Sidhu butchered the bowling. Suddenly, 270 did not seem too large. Srikkanth went for 70, but that only let Sidhu loose. As the experienced Dilip Vengsarkar played a mature knock, Sidhu hit five towering sixes which created a carnival atmosphere. At 207 for two, victory seemed a few blows away. The drama began. Soon the score was 265 for nine. With six runs left, 'Ice Man' Steve Waugh bowled the last over to Maninder Singh. The previous year's tied Test between the two teams at the same venue flashed into the mind. Maninder managed four off four balls. Two runs were needed. Off the fifth ball, Maninder was bowled. India lost by a solitary run.

Australia 270 for 6 wickets (50 overs)
India 269 all out (49.5 overs)

Calypso silenced

England v West Indies
Gujranwala, October 9, 1987

Allan Lamb

Was Vivian Richards' team good enough? The English were on unfamiliar territory. They met at the unlikely venue of Gujranwala. In an ominous start Carlisle Best was bowled by Philip DeFreitas at 8. Richie Richardson combined with Desmond Haynes and Vivian Richards in useful stands. Neil Foster bowled both Richardson and Richards. Jeff Dujon and Gus Logie added 83. The West Indies made 243 for seven off 50 overs. English wickets tumbled. Graham Gooch made 47. At 131 for six, England were in strife. Allan Lamb had only the tailenders for company. With 10 overs left, 91 runs were required. Lamb raised valuable runs in his forthright manner, with John Emburey and DeFreitas. With eight down, 35 runs were needed off 3 overs. Lamb was in top gear but it was still anyone's game. Lamb lashed 15 runs off Courney Walsh. Patrick Patterson conceded six runs. Off the last over 13 were required. Lamb despatched Walsh's full toss to the fence. A leg-side wide flew to the boundary. Lamb took a single off a no-ball. Foster hit the winning boundary. England snatched a thrilling win. Lamb's was a superb unbeaten 67 off 68 balls.

West Indies 243 for 7 wickets (50 overs)
England 246 for 8 wickets (49.3 overs)

Spanking shots 'n close shave

New Zealand v Zimbabwe
Hyderabad (I), October 10, 1987

David Houghton

Seamer Martin Snedden partnered John Wright. The Kiwis put on a bright 59. The classical stylist, Martin Crowe and Snedden added 84. Wickets started tumbling. They ended at 242 for seven in 50 overs. Zimbabwe were in trouble at 104 for seven. The cynics derided the abilities of the minor team. In no mood to allow the critics the satisfaction of seeing his team humiliated, David Houghton brought the somnolent crowd to life with a barrage of fours and sixes. He put on a record 117 runs with Iain Butchart. At 221, a shock victory was just 22 runs away. Then Houghton lofted Snedden. Martin Crowe ran against the flight, made a headlong dive and grabbed the precious spheroid, the catch of the tournament. Houghton's 142 off 137 balls contained 13 fours and 6 sixes, Zimbabwe's first-ever century. The tide turned. Last pair, Butchart and John Traicos added 18 runs amid unbearable tension. Four runs were required off three balls. Butchart was run out. Zimbabwe were stranded, wondering what might have been.

New Zealand 242 for 7 wickets (50 overs)
Zimbabwe 239 all out (49.4 overs)

Last ball drama

Pakistan v West Indies
Lahore, October 16, 1987

Courtney Walsh

This was a battle royale as former champions West Indies took on hot favourites, Pakistan. Desmond Haynes and Phil Simmons put on 91 runs. Simmons hit up a free-scoring half-century. The West Indies were bowled out for 216. Imran Khan finished with four for 37. Pakistan slipped to 110 for five off 35 overs. Salim Yousuf hit a belligerent 56. After 49 overs Pakistan were 203 for nine. Fourteen were required off the last over. Courtney Walsh had captured four for 26 runs in 9 overs. He came on for the last over. Four runs came off three balls. Abdul Qadir swiped a straight six. Four were needed off two balls. Qadir again ran two. Two were needed off the last ball. Walsh ran up to bowl. Salim Jaffer, in his excitement, backed up too far. Walsh did not run him out but nodded a warning. He came in again and Qadir swung. The batsmen ran for their lives and got those two runs. Pakistan won by one wicket off the last ball. Amid scenes of wild jubilation, Qadir was the hero of a most dramatic finish. The game had also seen another hero, Courtney Walsh, for his tremendous show of sportsmanship.

West Indies 216 all out (49.3 overs)
Pakistan 217 for 9 wickets (50 overs)

Fun after the rain

David Boon

Australia v New Zealand
Indore, October 19, 1987

Soggy conditions forced a delay, and the match was curtailed to 30-overs-a-side. Geoff Marsh went early, but David Boon and Dean Jones set about the bowling in a manner justified by the circumstances. They thrashed the ball all over as they raised 117 runs off 98 deliveries. Jones fell for 52 made in his usual bustling way off only 48 balls. Skipper Allan Border joined the carnival as Boon continued to blaze away. The chunky little opener was caught for 87 off 96 deliveries. Australia finished one short of the 200 runs mark off the allotted 30 overs. Ken Rutherford and John Wright put on 83. Then Andrew Jones helped Martin Crowe push the score along. Crowe scored a brilliant half-century and seemed to be guiding his side to an exciting win. Cool customer Steve Waugh took the ball with the Kiwis needing seven off the last over with four wickets in hand. The classy Crowe played an injudicious shot to be caught by Marsh. Ian Smith was bowled off the next ball, and Waugh ran out Martin Snedden. Suddenly it was 194 for nine. The six runs required proved too many for the last pair; they managed only two.

Australia 199 for 4 wickets (30 overs)
New Zealand 196 for 9 wickets (30 overs)

Indians struck by the blues

England v India
Perth (D/N), February 22, 1992

Robin Smith

The first ever day-night match in the World Cup saw skipper Graham Gooch taking along the imposing figure of Ian Botham to open the innings. The burly allrounder was dismissed soon. Another belligerent strokeplayer, Robin Smith added 110 with Gooch. The captain was dismissed for 51. One-day specialist, the left-handed Neil Fairbrother helped Smith add 60. Then the English innings fell away. Smith, who was careering down in top gear, crashed nine short of a ton. England scored 236 for nine. Krish Srikkanth, who made utter nonsense of the copybook on his day, and the resolute Ravi Shastri put on 63 in a stand reminiscent of their days of glory in 1985. Srikkanth departed for 39. Shastri and child prodigy Sachin Tendulkar doubled the score but India faded rapidly. England's other One-day specialist Dermot Reeve was incisive. Ian Botham's accurate bowling proved decisive. At 201 for nine only the rituals seemed to remain. Subroto Bannerjee and Javagal Srinath put on 26. Ten were needed off five balls. But Srinath was run out, the fourth in the innings.

England 236 for 9 wickets (50 overs)
India 227 all out (49.2 overs)

An appetite for runs

Sri Lanka v Zimbabwe
New Plymouth, February 23, 1992

Andy Flower

Pukekura Park was an unfamiliar venue in an equally strange New Zealand town of New Plymouth, about 260 kilometres north of the capital, Wellington. This rich dairy-farming region must have whetted the appetite of the batsmen, for they went on an unprecedented run-feast. Andy Flower batted through the innings, becoming the third to score a century on debut in One-dayers. Kevin Arnott scored a polished 52. The rampaging Andy Waller milked the bowling as the locals would their cows. He took only 32 balls to reach fifty and crashed 9 fours and 3 sixes in his unbeaten 83 off 45 balls. Flower and Waller put on an unbroken 145 runs for the fifth wicket, then a World Cup record. Zimbabwe hit their best One-day total of 312 for four. Roshan Mahanama and Athula Samarasekara put on 128. The urgency caused wickets to fall. Arjuna Ranatunga was a man for the big occasion. He played a pivotal role, timing the chase to a nicety. The enormous task was achieved in the last over. It was a superb unbeaten 88 from the rotund left-hander. Sri Lanka's 313 for seven is the highest for a team batting second in the World Cup.

Zimbabwe 312 for 4 wickets (50 overs)
Sri Lanka 313 for 7 wickets (49.2 overs)

That one run again

Australia v India
Brisbane, March 1, 1992

David Boon

The winners of the last two World Cups were having a lean time. Both were eager to perform well. Australia were jolted by Kapil Dev. David Boon and Dean Jones put on 71. Jones hit 90 off 108 balls. The Indian seamers got into the swing of things. From 230 for five, Australia slumped to 237 for nine in 50 overs. Then a flawed rule regarding interruption of play by rain began to cast a shadow. Three overs were lopped off the Indian innings. The target score was reduced by only 2 runs. Mohammad Azharuddin and Sanjay Manjrekar put on 66 for the fifth wicket. Azhar was run out for 93 off 103 balls. Tom Moody bowled the pulsating last over. India needed 13 with three wickets left. Kiran More flicked the first two balls for fours, then got carried away. His middle stump broke into two. The fourth ball produced a single. Manoj Prabhakar was run out off the fifth. Javagal Srinath swung hard but straight to Steve Waugh. He dropped the catch but quickly threw the ball back. Venkatapathy Raju was going for the run that would have tied the scores. The throw beat him. Australia won a dramatic match by 1 run.

Australia 237 for 9 wickets (50 overs)
India 234 all out (47 overs)

Skillful chase

South Africa v Sri Lanka
Wellington, March 2, 1992

Arjuna Ranatunga

Aravinda de Silva put South Africa in to bat in overcast, bitterly cold and blustery conditions. Kepler Wessels and Peter Kirsten added 87 for the second wicket. They were both dismissed at 114. By then 35.5 overs had already been bowled. South Africa needed to accelerate but they collapsed. The last nine wickets fell for 81 runs off 85 balls. They were all out for 195 off the final ball of the innings. Sri Lanka ran headlong into trouble. Allan Donald sent back Chandika Hathurusinghe, Asanka Gurusinha and de Silva. They collapsed to 35 for three in the ninth over. Donald had caused mayhem. Roshan Mahanama and Hashan Tillekeratne put on 54. Arjuna Ranatunga played a highly skilled innings. Mahanama reached his third fifty in as many innings in this World Cup. They took the score to 154. Mahanama departed for 68 off 121 deliveries. Two more wickets fell. At 189 for seven, the overs were running out. Donald bowled the last over. Ranatunga held firm. Sri Lanka grabbed a thrilling victory off the second-last ball. The crafty left-hander was unbeaten with 64 off 73 balls with six boundaries.

South Africa 195 all out (50 overs)
Sri Lanka 198 for 7 wickets (49.5 overs)

Rain-rule nearly plays spoilsport

England v South Africa
Melbourne (D/N), March 12, 1992

Kepler Wessels

The ungainly, but effective, Kepler Wessels and the technically accomplished Andrew Hudson gave South Africa a head start, putting on 151. Wessels scored 85 and Hudson 79. South Africa finished at 236 for four. Alec Stewart and Ian Botham batted merrily till the rain came at 62 for no loss off 12 overs. Nine overs were taken away, and the silly rule decreed that only 11 runs be reduced from the target-score. The big allrounder Brian McMillan bowled Botham, and had Robin Smith taken at the wicket. Richard Snell dismissed Graeme Hick similarly. England slumped to 64 for three. Neil Fairbrother showed once again why he is rated so high. And Alec Stewart has always been a cricketer of substance. They added 68 for the fourth wicket. Stewart was run out for 77 off 88 deliveries. Fairbrother added 34 with Dermot Reeve, and 50 with Chris Lewis, who smashed 33 off 22 deliveries. With canny grasp of the mechanics of batting in a One-day game, Fairbrother guided his side to victory with just one ball to spare.

South Africa 236 for 4 wickets (50 overs)
England 226 for 7 wickets (40.5 overs)

Zimbabwe ride better on bumpy track

England v Zimbabwe
Albury, March 18, 1992

Eddo Brandes

One of the fringe benefits that seemed to accrue from matches against Zimbabwe during those time were trips to upcountry locations. The English must have come to Albury - on the Murray river and lying on the major route between Sydney and Melbourne - for a breath of fresh air and a regulation win. Instead, what they encountered was a fresh wicket and a fiery Eddo Brandes. The pitch afforded plenty of bounce and movement. David Houghton put together all his skills to conjure a well-compiled 29. Zimbabwe got as far as 134. The chunky Brandes trapped Graham Gooch leg-before with the scoreboard still blank. Ian Botham and Allan Lamb eked out 32 runs. Disaster was always round the corner in this game. England got into a mess at 43 for five. Brandes had taken four for 16. Neil Fairbrother and Alec Stewart put on 52. At 108 for eight, England looked doomed. Richard Illingworth and Gladstone Small added 16. Ten runs were required by the last pair in the final over. Small was caught off the first ball. England slumped to a sensational defeat. For the jubilant Zimbabweans it was their second victory in the World Cup.

Zimbabwe 134 all out (46.1 overs)
England 125 all out (49.1 overs)

Bubble bursts eventually

England v South Africa (semi final)
Sydney (D/N), March 22, 1992

Graeme Hick

It is said that the game of cricket often makes fools of even the masters. The experts who made the already infamous rule regarding reduction of overs due to interference by the weather, were made to look silly. The utterly foolish rule was seen in all its magnified ignominy here, and it mined an exciting match. Graeme Hick played a glorious innings, stroking 83 off 90 deliveries. England notched up 252 for six in an innings shortened by five overs. South African opener Andrew Hudson, hard-hitting allrounder Adrian Kuiper, and the unorthodox Jonty Rhodes made a match of it. Gladstone Small created a minor flutter getting two important wickets in the middle. At 206 for six, Brian McMillan was joined by Dave Richardson. They added 25 priceless runs and were still together with just 22 required off 13 deliveries. Down came the rain. When play resumed, the authorities decreed that South Africa had only one delivery left to score those 22 runs. It could not be a more tragi-comic situation. Also, instead of allowing such a ridiculous situation, surely the remaining two overs could have been bowled.

England 252 for 6 wickets (45 overs)
South Africa 232 for 6 wickets (43 overs)

Black day for Caribbeans

Kenya v West Indies
Pune, February 29, 1996

Maurice Odumbe

The early life in the wicket suited the West Indies pacemen, as they went about skittling the Kenyans. Lanky off-spinner Roger Harper also got into the act and Kenya were reduced to 81 for six. Only a face-saving 44-run stand between left-handed Hitesh Modi and 18-year-old Thomas Odoyo gave some respectability to the score. But they were all out for a paltry 166 in 49.3 overs. It was not a score that was liable to test the Caribbean line-up. The West Indians, however, can be an unpredictable lot. If Kenya had made a bad start, the West Indies innings never took off. Richie Richardson went for 5, the great Brian Lara for 8, both consumed by Rajab Ali. Shivanaraine Chanderpaul tried to graft, as is his wont, but Keith Arthurton, who had a nightmarish tournament, contrived to get himself run out for a duck. Man-of-the-match Maurice Odumbe came on with his off-breaks, and tore through the middle-order. At 78 for seven, it was a hopeless situation. The inevitable happened as Rajab Ali returned to claim last-man Cameron Cuffy, his third successive three-wicket haul. The West Indies crashed to 93 all out. They had reached the nadir.

Kenya 166 all out (49.3 overs)
West Indies 93 all out (35.2 overs)

Lankans zip through

India v Sri Lanka
New Delhi, March 2, 1996

Sanath Jayasuriya

Sachin Tendulkar was superb. He did not blast away from the outset, for the importance of the match was not lost on him. Sanjay Manjrekar, though not pedestrian, was sedate as usual. The Mumbai lads put on 66 off 82 deliveries for the second wicket. Tendulkar changed gears. He had taken 72 balls to get his first 50. The second fifty took only 50 balls. Then he went berserk, scoring at over two runs per ball. He put on 175 with Mohommad Azharuddin in only 26 overs. His 137 with 5 sixes and 8 fours came at a-run-a-ball. Azharuddin scored 72 not out off 80 balls. A target of 272 was stiff even for rising stars. That is if it is measured by an ordinary yardstick. In 1996 the Lankans were no ordinary side. Sanath Jayasuriya and Romesh Kaluwitharana put on 53 in 5 overs. Manoj Prabhakar bore the brunt, being hit for 33 runs in two overs. Kaluwitharana went for 26. The momentum was kept up. After 10 overs the score was 82; after 15 it was 119. Jayasuriya blazed away to 79 off 76 balls. The asking-rate crashed below 4.75 per over with 131 runs needed. Arjuna Ranatunga and Hashan Tillekeratne reached their goal with 8 balls to spare.

India 271 for 3 wickets (50 overs)
Sri Lanka 272 for 4 wickets (48.4 overs)

Antipodeans score

Australia v New Zealand (quarter-final)
Madras (D/N), March 11, 1996

Lee Germon

Hot and steamy Madras, now known as Chennai, is an unlikely venue for a protracted battle but it invariably produces exciting cricket. At 44 for three the Kiwis were in trouble. Lee Germon and Chris Harris set about the Aussie bowling. The World Cup record for the fourth wicket fell as they added 168 runs in just 27 overs. They surpassed the 149 put on by Clive Lloyd and Rohan Kanhai in the 1975 final. Germon's 89 came off 96 balls. Harris hit a maiden century in his 62nd One-dayer. His 130 was scored off 124 deliveries with 13 fours and 4 sixes. A score of 286 seemed awesome. Mark Waugh added 65 for the second wicket with Ricky Ponting. Pinch-hitter Shane Warne swiped 24 off just 14 balls. Twin Steve joined Mark Waugh. Their partnership was worth 86. Mark hit a magnificent 110 off 112 deliveries, the first to score three centuries in a single World Cup. The asking rate was still 7 per over. Steve Waugh and Stuart Law assumed charge and hit up the 74 needed with 13 balls to spare. Law crashed 42 off 30 balls, while Steve Waugh's 59 came off 68 deliveries.

New Zealand 286 for 9 wickets (50 overs)
Australia 289 for 4 wickets (47.5 overs)

So near, yet.....

Shane Warne

Australia v West Indies (semi-final)
Mohali (D/N), March 14, 1996

Even in decline the West Indies were not a side to be trifled with. Curtly Ambrose trapped Mark Waugh leg-before with the second ball of the match. Mark Taylor, Ricky Ponting and Steve Waugh also left soon. It was a disaster at 15 for four after 9.1 overs. Run-by-run Stuart Law and Michael Bevan built up the innings. They posted an Australian fifth-wicket World Cup record stand of 138 runs. Law was run out for 72. Bevan departed for 69. Ian Healy hit 31 off 28 balls. A score of 207 was not too large. Shivnaraine Chanderpaul and Brian Lara batted untroubled. Lara scored 45 at a run-a-ball. Richie Richardson filled the breach admirably. Chanderpaul holed out for 80. Another 43 were required off 50 balls. Five wickets fell in a heap. Shane Warne was spinning his magic. The West Indies needed 10 off the final over. Richardson blasted the first ball for four. Ambrose was run out. Courtney Walsh had no idea about what he was supposed to do. The ball crashed into his stumps. The West Indies had been in control for 91 overs. They did not know how to handle the final nine.

Australia 207 for 8 wickets (50 overs)
West Indies 202 all out (49.3 overs)

A tragedy for India

India v Zimbabwe
Leicester, May 19,1999

Henry Olonga

This match was to haunt India throughout the tournament and, in fact, eventually led to their exit without making it to the last four stage. India seemed to have had the match wrapped up after two fighting partnerships. Robin Singh put on 44 for the seventh wicket with Nayan Mongia, and another 27 for the eighth wicket with Javagal Srinath. With two overs left there were only 9 runs to get with three wickets in hand. Just the formalities remained, or so it seemed. Speedster Henry Olonga, who had bowled only three uninspiring overs, was brought on. He dismissed Robin Singh with his second ball, caught by skipper Alistair Campbell for 35. Srinath, who had crashed 18 off 12 balls including 2 sixes, made a horrible swipe only to have his stumps shattered. Off the last ball of his over, Olonga trapped Venkatesh Prasad plumb in front. Zimbabwe pulled off an incredible win by three runs. It was a very sad day for India. Their star batsman Sachin Tendulkar had earlier flown home following the sudden demise of his father. They then conceded a World Cup record 51 extras, and were also docked four overs as a result of their slow over-rate. On some days nothing goes right. This was one such.

Zimbabwe 252 for 9 wickets (50 overs)
India 249 all out (45 overs)

Pakistan on a high

Australia v Pakistan
Leeds, May 23, 1999

Inzamam-ul-Haq

Powered by an entertaining 81 by Inzamam-ul-Haq and
scintillating hitting by the lower middle order, Pakistan posted
an imposing 275 for eight. Australia, despite a fine 91-run
second-wicket stand between Mark Waugh (41) and Ricky
Ponting (47), slumped to 101 for four. Skipper Steve Waugh
and Michael Bevan resurrected the innings with a fine 113-
run partnership. There were now 62 runs required off 52 balls
with 6 wickets in hand. The brilliant Pakistani captain Wasim
Akram took matters into his own hands. Having already played
a quickfire knock and dismissed Adam Gilchrist for a duck,
Akram effected the vital breakthrough by having Bevan caught
by Ijaz Ahmed. The pacy Shoaib Akhtar then went through
Steve Waugh's defence and the door was wide open. There was
not much resistance from the tail. Akram mopped up the last
two wickets and with 540 runs scored in nearly 100 overs, the
difference was just 10 runs. Pakistan took first points in the
battle of the titans.

Pakistan 275 for 8 wickets (50 overs)
Australia 265 all out (49.5 overs)

Proteas back with a bang

Pakistan v South Africa
Nottingham, June 5, 1999

Lance Klusener

One of the highlights of the 1999 World Cup was the sustained brilliance of Lance Klusener. He exploded into one of the most amazing strikers of the cricket ball. Already he was unbeaten in the four innings that he had played in the tournament. He came in at 135 for six with South Africa needing 86 to win. When Jacques Kallis fell at 176, 45 were needed off 34 balls with just three wickets in hand. But 'Zulu' Klusener was like a man possessed. He launched a ferocious attack, and found an able ally in Mark Boucher. Bowlers of the likes of Wasim Akram, Shoaib Akhtar and Saqlain Mushtaq had no answer. Klusener and Boucher put on 45 off just 28 balls in their undefeated stand. South Africa were home with an over to spare. Klusener struck 46 off 41 balls with 3 sixes and 3 fours. Earlier another star of this World Cup, Moin Khan, had given his team a fair chance of a win with a typically belligerent 63 off 56 balls. Then the pacemen reduced the South African innings to shambles, having them on the mat at 58 for five. They did not reckon with Klusener.

Pakistan 220 for 7 wickets (50 overs)
South Africa 221 for 7 wickets (49 overs)

Waugh zone

Australia v South Africa
Leeds, June 13, 1999

Steve Waugh

Sometimes it takes just one silly slip to turn a hero into a villian, and to offer that tiny spur to an opponent to break free and deliver the *coup-de-grace*. Herschelle Gibbs had been the man of the moment for South Africa with his superb 101. Jonty Rhodes and Lance Klusener thrashed the ball around at the end. Australia desperately needed to win in order to advance into the semi-finals. Facing a daunting target of 272, they were precariously placed at 48 for three. Ricky Ponting and Steve Waugh began their uphill battle. It was intriguing cricket. At 152 the ship had been steadied. Waugh flicked one straight to Gibbs at short mid-wicket. Gibbs pouched it easily and in his excitement to hurl it in the air, the ball slipped. Waugh was then 56. Men like him need just that stroke of luck. He dug in his heels as he knows best. The score started climbing with Steve Waugh playing one of the most outstanding innings of his glittering career. Still, it was an extremely close affair. There were 8 runs to win when the last over began. The Aussies need not have worried. Waugh brought up victory in the company of Tom Moody with two deliveries to spare. It was a terrific display.

South Africa 271 for 7 wickets (50 overs)
Australia 272 for 5 wickets (49.4 overs)

Sensational tie

Australia v South Africa (semi-final)
Birmingham, June 17, 1999

Shane Warne

This was perhaps the most exciting match in World Cup history. Shaun Pollock and Allan Donald bowled superbly. Australia managed only 213 runs. Steve Waugh and Michael Bevan put on 90 for the fifth wicket, both hitting half-centuries. South Africa slipped to 61 for four. Jacques Kallis, Jonty Rhodes and Pollock retrieved the situation. Wickets fell even as Lance Klusener began his pyrotechnics. With 4 overs left, another 30 were needed. Klusener drove one over Paul Reiffel who palmed it across the boundary. Nine were needed off the final over with the last pair in. Klusener hammered two rasping fours. The scores were tied. Steve Waugh brought all his fielders in. Donald was almost run out off the third ball. He decided not to run next ball. Klusener did. Then Donald ran minus his bat. There was enough time for the Aussies to relay the ball from short cover to the bowler's end to the wicketkeeper. It was a tie, the first in the World Cup. Australia were through to the final having beaten South Africa earlier.

Australia 213 all out (49.2 overs)
South Africa 213 all out (49.4 overs)

Prince and the tortoise

South Africa v West Indies
Cape Town (D/N), February 9, 2003

Brian Lara

Brian Lara delighted with a century of pure genius. But South Africa paid for their slow over-rate, being docked one priceless over. The tentative Chris Gayle and Wavell Hinds were scoreless off the first three overs. By the time the score crawled to seven, Shaun Pollock had put both out of their misery. Lara stepped in at 4 for one. Jacques Kallis dropped him first ball at second slip off Makhaya Ntini. West Indies lurched to 12 for two after 10 overs. Lara went into overdrive. He put on 102 with Shivnaraine Chanderpaul and 89 with Carl Hooper. Lara departed after a stunning 116 off 134 balls with 12 fours and 2 sixes. Ricardo Powell and Ramnaresh Sarwan fired the final shots, adding 63. Pollock was smashed for 23 runs off one over. The hosts faltered, slipping to 160 for six. Mark Boucher led a revival along with Lance Klusener. Boucher fell for 49 at a-run-a-ball. Klusener and Nicky Boje put on 67. Klusener was on strike with 8 runs to win off four balls. But he holed out. His 57 off 48 balls was in vain. South Africa lost by three runs.

West Indies 278 for five wickets (50 overs)
South Africa 275 for nine wickets (49 overs)

Skipper's saga

New Zealand v South Africa
Johannesburg, February 16, 2003

Stephen Fleming

Herschelle Gibbs hit a dazzling century to help South Africa post a 300-plus total but, as at Headingley in 1999, it was overshadowed by a match-winning hundred from the opposing skipper. There was another similarity. In that match four years earlier, Gibbs had blundered with a catch offered by ultimate centurion Steve Waugh, when on 56. Here, wicketkeeper Mark Boucher grassed a dolly nicked by Stephen Fleming, batting on 53. History does repeat itself. Gibbs raised half-century stands for the first four wickets, hitting up 143 off 141 balls with 19 fours and 3 sixes. Lance Klusener smashed 33 off 21 deliveries. Bad light and rain caused two stoppages; there was even a power failure. The Duckworth-Lewis method set a target of 226 in 39 overs. Fleming and Craig McMillan raised 89. Fleming played one of the great innings of the World Cup, and clinched an easy victory against difficult odds. Nathan Astle was his ally in a stand of 140. Fleming was unbeaten with 134 off 132 balls, having hit 21 fours. South Africans were stunned.

South Africa 306 for six wickets (50 overs)
New Zealand 229 for one wicket (36.5 overs)

A Kenyan wrong 'un

Kenya v Sri Lanka
Nairobi, February 24, 2003

Collins Obuya

Leg-spinner Collins Obuya helped hosts Kenya upset Sri Lanka. Hitherto his nine wickets in 18 One-day Internationals had cost 78.22 each. But at Nairobi, the lanky Obuya churned out the second-best figures for a spinner in the World Cup, behind fellow African leggie Paul Strang's five for 21. It was a shock reminiscent of their victory over the West Indies in 1996. Kenyan batting drew its impetus from Kennedy Otieno's resilient 60, and they crossed 200. Hashan Tillekeratne and veteran Aravinda de Silva battled for Sri Lanka but Obuya had the former taken in the deep. Mahela Jayawardene hit back a catch to Obuya. Otieno lunged forward to catch Kumar Sangakkara, helping his brother claim another wicket. De Silva finally nicked Obuya into Otieno's gloves. Chaminda Vaas was caught and bowled by Obuya. From 71 for two, Sri Lanka slumped to 119 for seven. Obuya finished with five for 24, the best-ever for Kenya. Sri Lanka crashed to 157 all out. Kenya made it to the super-six, and then amazingly to the semi-finals.

Kenya 210 for nine wickets (50 overs)
Sri Lanka 157 all out (45 overs)

Windies pipped at the outpost

Sri Lanka v West Indies
Cape Town (D/N), February 28, 2003

Ramnaresh Sarwan

Sanath Jayasuriya won a significant toss but Sri Lanka could not accelerate. Jayasuriya and Hashan Tillekeratne added 85. Aravinda de Silva was in vintage form but was run out in a silly mix-up. Jayasuriya fell for 66 off 99 balls. The strong West Indies line-up faced a moderate target but the in-form Chaminda Vaas struck early. Brian Lara was scoreless for 17 deliveries, then nearly ran himself out. Vaas had him caught behind for 1. Dilhara Fernando hit Ramnaresh Sarwan on the head, putting him in hospital, and trapped Hooper leg-before. Shivnaraine Chanderpaul raised 59 with Chris Gayle. Vaas had Gayle leg-before for 55, and dismissed Ridley Jacobs too. Muttiah Muralitharan sent back Ricardo Powell. Chanderpaul and Vasbert Drakes put on 47. The courageous Sarwan strode in and began hitting out. Runs flowed. Fourteen were needed off 2 overs. Muralitharan conceded just 2 runs in the 49th over. West Indies could not pull it off. Sarwan was unbeaten with 47 off 44 balls. South Africans rejoiced. This result gave them a chance to bid for the super-six.

Sri Lanka 228 for six wickets (50 overs)
West Indies 222 for nine wickets (50 overs)

Aussies never say never

Australia v England
Port Elizabeth, March 2, 2003

Andy Bichel

It was a classic contest. England openers Nick Knight and Marcus Trescothick raced to 50 off 7.1 overs. At 66, Andy Bichel had Knight caught at gully. Next over, he had Michael Vaughan caught behind, and castled Nasser Hussain. Glenn McGrath removed Trescothick. Bichel had Paul Collingwood nicking to Adam Gilchrist. England lost five wickets for 19. Alec Stewart and Andrew Flintoff put on 90. Bichel had Flintoff snapped up by Gilchrist, and bowled Stewart. He added Giles to his bag of seven for 20, second-best in the World Cup. Andy Caddick picked up Matthew Hayden, and then Gilchrist. He trapped Damien Martyn for a duck and dismissed Ricky Ponting. Australia reeled at 48 for four. Darren Lehmann and Michael Bevan battled, yet at 114 for seven they were pensive. 'Terminator' Bevan and Bichel dug in but the asking-rate rose. With 14 runs to get off 2 overs, Bichel clouted James Anderson for 11 runs. Bevan brought up victory in the final over. The stand was worth 73 runs off 74 balls, a stupendous turnaround.

England 204 for eight wickets (50 overs)
Australia 208 for eight wickets (49.4 overs)

South Africa's night of horror

South Africa v Sri Lanka
Durban (D/N), March 3, 2003

Marvan Atapattu

South Africa desperately needed a win, Sri Lanka only a good run-rate. Marvan Atapattu was in sublime form. Neither Sanath Jayasuriya's run out nor the regular fall of wickets bothered him. He drove three boundaries in Shaun Pollock's second over. Aravinda de Silva joined up at 90 for three in the 23rd over. They scored at near a-run-a-ball. Atapattu brought up a chanceless hundred. Reaching a delightful fifty, de Silva hoisted two sixes. The 152-run stand virtually ensured a super-six berth. Atapattu hit 124 off 129 balls with 18 fours, and de Silva 73 off 78 balls with 6 fours and the two sixes. Herschelle Gibbs and Graeme Smith put on 65 runs in 11 overs. Lankan spinners reduced the Proteas to 149 for five. Mark Boucher and Pollock added 63. With rain around, Boucher was told that the victory target, by the Duckworth-Lewis method, after 45 overs was 229. Muttiah Muralitharan was hit for 13 runs off five balls of that fateful over. Boucher blocked the last delivery. The rain came. South Africa were horrified to learn that they had only tied the match.

Sri Lanka 268 for nine wickets (50 overs)
South Africa 229 for six wickets (45 overs)

Africans love ties

Ireland v Zimbabwe
Kingston, March 15, 2007

Jeremy Bray

Only Stuart Matsikenyeri had appeared once in the World Cup. He was at the bottom of the Zimbabwe averages, batting and bowling. Ireland were making their debut. William Porterfield was dismissed on a greenish wicket by Chris Mpofu for zero. Left-hander Jeremy Bray played a power-packed innings. Eoin Morgan and Andrew White featured in useful stands. Bray completed a superb century, emulating Glenn Turner, Andy Flower, Gary Kirsten and Craig Wishart by carrying his bat on Cup debut. His unbeaten 115 off 137 balls with 10 fours and a six saw Ireland to 221 for nine. Zimbabwean Vusimuzi Sibanda scored a fine 67. At 203 for five, just 19 were needed off 27 deliveries. Suddenly, Taylor was run out. Gary Brent consumed 12 deliveries over 3 runs. Skipper Prosper Utseya and Mpofu lost their wickets. Zimbabwe were 213 for nine after 49 overs. Matsikenyeri took five runs off three deliveries. Edward Rainsford returned the strike. Matsikenyeri scored two off the fifth to level the scores. He failed to connect the final ball, then Rainsford was run out. It was the third tie in the World Cup, all involving an African team.

Ireland 221 for nine wickets (50 overs)
Zimbabwe 221 all out (50 overs)

Big Brother sent staggering

Bangladesh v India
Port of Spain, March 17, 2007

Mashrafe Mortaza

The pacy Mashrafe Mortaza revelled in seaming conditions. Virender Sehwag chopped his off-cutter onto the stumps. Mortaza moved one away; Robin Uthappa slashed to point. Tendulkar edged Abdur Razzak into Mushfiqur Rahim's gloves. Skipper Rahul Dravid trudged back at 72 for four. Only Yuvraj Singh fired, hitting 47 off 58 balls. India floundered at 159 for nine. Old-fashioned swipes by Zaheer Khan and the unlikely Munaf Patel helped raise 191. Mortaza's four for 38 shattered India; left-arm spinners Razzak and Mohammad Rafique mopped up. Shahriar Nafees returned cheaply. Tamim Iqbal smashed 7 fours and 2 sixes in his 53-ball 51. Mushfiqur and Shakib Al Hasan added 84. Shakib fell for 53 but Mushfiqur clinched victory with his unbeaten 56. Not since their defeat by Sri Lanka in 1979 had India suffered such humiliation. Already rocked by Greg Chappell's controversial coaching stint, this was disaster. For Bangladesh it provided exciting possibilities. Suddenly the plot took unexpected turns. The next few hours were even more astounding. No cricket World Cup had provided such drama.

India 191 all out (49.3 overs)
Bangladesh 192 for five wickets (48.3 overs)

Surprise and horror

Ireland v Pakistan
Kingston, March 17, 2007

Niall O'Brien

Cricket had not seen a more topsy-turvy and tragic turn of events. Two evenings earlier, debutants Ireland figured in an exhilarating last-ball tie with Zimbabwe. On this fateful day, Bangladesh upset India, and rank outsiders Ireland outplayed Pakistan. If the cricket world was stunned, it was devastated when Pakistani coach Bob Woolmer was found dead in his hotel next morning. A long, black shadow eclipsed all the splendid cricket. Trent Johnston put Pakistan in on a green-top. There was no half-century partnership, and no one touched 30; extras top-scoring with 29. They crashed for 132. Seamers Boyd Rankin and Andre Botha returned with three for 32 and 8-4-5-2 respectively, while off-spinner Kyle McCallan grabbed two for 12. Mohammad Sami trapped Jeremy Bray and Eoin Morgan leg-before-wicket cheaply but the southpaw stumper Niall 'Paddy' O'Brien hit 72 of the 93 runs scored while he was in. Younger brother Kevin brought up a sensational three-wicket win. A pensive Woolmer quietly packed away his computer that had become such an integral part of his stints as coach. That was the last image of this gutsy gentleman cricketer.

Pakistan 132 all out (45.4 overs)
Ireland 133 for seven wickets (41.4 overs)

Four-in-four…..
and then a streaky four

South Africa v Sri Lanka
Providence, March 28, 2007

Lasith Malinga

Charl Langeveldt struck two early blows. Herschelle Gibbs flew into the stumps Jonty Rhodes-style to effect a run out. Tillakaratne Dilshan and Russel Arnold added 97. The last five Sri Lankan wickets tumbled for 14. Langeveldt bagged five for 39. Chaminda Vaas castled Abraham de Villiers for zero. Graeme Smith raised a-run-a-ball fifty. Jacques Kallis and Gibbs added 65. Magical Murali took a smart return catch to dismiss Gibbs, and trapped Mark Boucher leg-before first ball. Four runs were required off 32 deliveries with five wickets left. Lasith Malinga's pin-point yorker scattered Shaun Pollock's timber. Next ball, Andrew Hall lobbed another slower one to cover. That ended 'Slinger' Malinga's over. One run was scored off the next. Kallis faced Malinga's hat-trick ball. The perky little paceman had him caught behind, the fifth World Cup hat-trick, emulating Chetan Sharma, Saqlain Mushtaq, Vaas and Brett Lee. Another Malinga yorker whistled into Makhaya Ntini's stumps. He snatched four wickets in four balls. It was 207 for nine. Eleven deliveries produced a single, but Robin Peterson edged Malinga to the boundary. South Africa were home, only just.

Sri Lanka 209 all out (49.3 overs)
South Africa 212 for nine wickets (48.2 overs)

See-saw comes up the right way for Lanka now

England v Sri Lanka
North Sound, April 4, 2007

Ravi Bopara

Sri Lanka had featured in a last-wicket drama. Now they starred in a last-ball thriller. Sanath Jayasuriya struck 4 fours and a six in his 26-ball 25. Paceman Sajid Mahmood dismissed him and Kumar Sangakkara. Upul Tharanga and Mahela Jayawardene strung 91. Andrew Flintoff prised out three key wickets. Sri Lanka folded up for 235. Sajid bagged four for 50. Chaminda Vaas had Michael Vaughan caught behind for a duck. Lasith Malinga dismissed Ed Joyce. England floundered at 11 for two. Ian Bell (47) and Kevin Pietersen (58) added 90. Dilhara Fernando struck two vital blows. Ravi Bopara and Paul Nixon battled. Nixon reverse-swept the great Muralitharan for a six and a four. Nineteen were needed off two overs. Malinga conceded just three runs in four balls, and removed Nixon off the fifth. Bopara cover-drove the last for a four. Twelve runs were required off the final over by the mercurial Fernando. Bopara scooped one the fine leg boundary. Three were required off the last ball. Bopara backed away to make room, Fernando bailed out. Bopara stepped away again, the ball crashed into the stumps. Sri Lanka pulled off a two-run win this time.

Sri Lanka 235 all out (50 overs)
England 233 for eight wickets (50 overs)

Tigers maul the Proteas

Bangladesh v South Africa
Providence, April 7, 2007

Mohammad Ashraful

Bangladesh had stunned India. Thereafter they looked out of place, but shone again now. Despite a fiery burst by the intractable Andre Nel, Mohammad Ashraful played one of his finest innings, highest for Bangladesh, which helped hoist their biggest total, in the World Cup. Nel struck thrice as Bangladesh slumped to 84 for four. Ashraful and Aftab Ahmed added 76. Aftab struck 2 sixes and 2 fours in his 35. Ashraful and Mashrafe Mortaza smashed 54 off 31 deliveries. Mortaza's 25 came off 16 balls. Ashraful fell for a brilliant 87 in 83 deliveries, having cracked a dozen boundaries. Nel dismissed both, finishing with five for 45. The final 47 balls yielded 72 runs. Left-arm seamer Syed Rasel dismissed Graeme Smith and Jacques Kallis. South Africa slumped to 87 for six. Uncertain running between wickets completed a dismal tale. Southpaw spinners Abdur Razzak, Mohammad Rafique and Shakib Al Hasan spun a web on this slow wicket, sharing six scalps. Herschelle Gibbs played a lone hand with an unbeaten 56 off 59 deliveries. It was one of the most glorious moments in Bangladesh cricket, trouncing the world's top One-day side by a whopping 67 runs.

Bangladesh 251 for eight wickets (50 overs)
South Africa 184 all out (48.4 overs)

Capricious giant-killers surprise once more

Bangladesh v Ireland
Bridgetown, April 15, 2007

William Porterfield

The minnows created a flutter in this event. Here were two teams that knocked out India and Pakistan. This match was remarkably similar to Bangladesh's upset of South Africa eight days earlier; but this time they were at the receiving end. Ireland had played with enthusiasm and gumption, and when they saw a chance to notch up another victory, they went for it with all the firepower at their command. William Porterfield and Jeremy Bray raised 92. Bray was run out for 31, the first of four such dismissals. Porterfield found another ally in Kevin O'Brien. The left-handed opener fell for 85 off 136 balls. Skipper Trent Johnston helped the younger O'Brien accelerate the scoring-rate. O'Brien hit up 48 off 44 balls, and Johnston clouted 30 from 23 deliveries as Ireland thrived. They posted their highest World Cup total. The Bangladesh innings hardly gained momentum on this dry pitch. Mohammad Ashraful (35) and Habibul Bashar (32) top-scored. All the Irish bowlers chipped in. Johnston his bit with his medium-pace too, taking two for 40. Bangladesh crashed to a humiliating 74-run defeat. It was a wonderful team effort that won the day for Ireland. Their enthusiasm and passion were a delight.

Ireland 243 for seven wickets (50 overs)
Bangladesh 169 all out (41.2 overs)

Exhilarating note to Lara's swansong

England v West Indies
Bridgetown, April 21, 2007

Kevin Pietersen

Neither side could enter the semi-finals but it was Brian Lara's farewell. For the first time a sell-out crowd converged. Chris Gayle hammered fifty off 29 balls. His 79 off 58 deliveries contained 10 fours and 3 sixes. Devon Smith helped post 131 upfront. Lara received a gracious guard of honour from the English. A vintage square-drive had the crowd on its feet. He had stroked 3 fours in his 18 off 17 balls. Marlon Samuels changed his call. Kevin Pietersen's direct hit found the legend short. There was a prolonged standing ovation. Samuels plundered 51 off 39 deliveries. West Indies totalled 300. Michael Vaughan took three for 39, then added 90 with Ravi Bopara in his classy 79 off 68 balls. Pietersen and Paul Nixon collected 80. Pietersen reached his century off 90 deliveries but was bowled instantly. The equation was 29 runs, three overs, two wickets. Nixon hit 3 fours off four deliveries, the fifth yielded four byes. Four runs were required in the last over. Dwayne Bravo castled Nixon. Two were needed from two balls with the last pair in. Stuart Broad swung the penultimate one over cover into the pickets. Lara's last words to the crowd were, "Did I entertain?".

West Indies 300 all out (49.5 overs)
England 301 for nine wickets (49.5 overs)

Star Turns

Star Turns

Stunning blows by Dennis Lillee

Dennis Lillee

Leeds, June 7, 1975

Dennis Lillee opened the bowling with Jeff Thomson as Pakistan set out in pursuit of the Australian score of 278 for seven. The legendary pair soon delivered a twin blow as Lillee made a mess of Sadiq Mohammad's stumps and Thomson had the struggling Zaheer Abbas snapped up. But at 181 for four, Pakistan seemed to be on target. Ian Chappell brought back Lillee and the great fast bowler immediately went through the defence of Asif Iqbal, who had played a captain's knock of 53. With Max Walker chipping in with the wickets of Wasim Raja and Imran Khan, Lillee demolished the tail in next to no time. He had Sarfraz Nawaz caught by comrade-in-arms, Rodney Marsh, for a duck. It was then the turn of Wasim Bari to be taken behind by his opposite number. Lillee put the final seal on the match by dismissing Asif Masood. Yet again he had turned a match with a devastating burst. Pakistan lost their last six wickets for just 24 runs, crashing to 205 all out. Lillee returned with a bag of five for 34 off his 12 overs, the first five-wicket haul in the World Cup. It was another proof that he belonged to the pantheon of the finest fast bowlers.

Alvin Kallicharran plays scintillating knock

Kennington Oval, London, June 14, 1975

Alvin Kallicharran

It was not a wicket on which batsmen had enjoyed themselves - till the diminutive Alvin Kallicharran walked in to take charge of the situation. Australia had been able to muster only 192 runs in 53.4 overs, and the West Indies had lost Gordon Greenidge for 16. A smooth-stroking left-hander, Kallicharran was not one to be contained for long. And what a bewildering assault he launched on one of the greatest fast bowlers in history, Dennis Lillee. The faster Lillee bowled, the harder did Kallicharran smash him. In a stunning sequence Kalli hit Lillee for 4.4.4.4.4.1.4.6.0.4 - 35 runs off 10 consecutive deliveries, driving and hooking brilliantly. He had the entire house on its feet, and left those glued to the radio or television wishing they were there. Kallicharran added 124 for the second wicket with opener Roy Fredericks to put the match beyond the Aussies. Kallicharran hit up a superb 78 off 83 balls with 14 fours and a six before Lillee finally had his revenge. He mishooked a bumper to be caught at mid-wicket by Ashley Mallet. This was vintage Kallicharran in an unforgettable innings. His keen eye and lightning footwork enabled him to get into position very early to execute his exciting strokes. While other batsmen struggled, Kallicharran sparkled. Truly one of the gems of the World Cup.

Kallicharran sparkles again

Alvin Kallicharran

Kennington Oval, London, June 18, 1975

After a scathing assault on a classy Australian attack, Alvin Kallicharran was ready and waiting for the Kiwis in a semi-final clash. The memory of his brilliant innings just four days earlier, and a modest target-score had the little Caribbean left-hander walking in a relaxed mode to join Gordon Greenidge. They put the attack to the sword in contrasting styles. Greenidge, one of the hardest hitters the game has known, was for the most part, put in the shade by Kallicharran's sparkling display. They put on 125 for the second wicket as the match quickly slipped away from the hapless New Zealanders. Kallicharran scored a delightful 72, timing his shots in exquisite fashion. He hit 7 fours and a six, displaying once again that he was one of the most exciting batsmen at that point in history. He was always elegant to watch. Whether he played a fierce hook or a rasping drive, the stroke never seemed to lack finesse. It looked as though Kalli just caressed the ball, sending it on its inevitable path to the boundary. His batting was as sunny as his disposition, and his antics on the field made him a favourite of the crowd.

Awesome century by Gordon Greenidge

Gordon Greenidge

Birmingham, June 9, 1979

Not for nothing was Gordon Greenidge known as one of the hardest hitters in the game. He was also technically accomplished, as India found to their chagrin. Greenidge was in splendid nick right from the first delivery. He played blazing shots to all parts of the ground, scorching the turf as the ball sped to the fence. Desmond Haynes, the other half of one of the finest opening partnerships in the annals of the game, kept him company in a century stand. It was, nevertheless, Greenidge's day as he hammered 6 fours on his way to a half-century off 72 deliveries. At tea it was 88 for no loss off 25 overs, with Greenidge 51 not out and Haynes on 30. They raised their century stand in the 29th over and carried the score to 138 before Haynes fell. It was only a case of frying pan to the fire for the Indian attack as Vivian Richards helped Greenidge wrap up the match. The rampaging Greenidge powered on to reach his century off 153 deliveries, hitting 9 fours and a six. He returned undefeated with 106 runs to his name, his maiden hundred in the competition. Greenidge combined the West Indian flair that he was born into, with technical competence that he acquired in the English system.

The bludgeon that was Clive Lloyd's bat

Nottingham, June 16, 1979

Clive Lloyd

Clive Lloyd would hit the ball with such explosive power that a fielder who ventured to stop it would virtually be thrown back a few yards. Here was another day when he put his awesome prowess on display. Lloyd had settled down to play his usual attacking innings. But at 204 for seven after 55 overs, the West Indies did not seem to have had enough runs on the board. That was when Lloyd shifted gears. He had only tailenders for company, but that did not bother Lloyd. He made a mess of the Kiwi attack, hammering it all over the park. Of the 40 priceless runs that he added in the last five overs, his partner Joel Garner contributed all of 9 runs. This helped carry the total to 244 after 60 overs. The West Indies were now on a stronger wicket. Lloyd had hit a blistering unbeaten 73 off 80 deliveries. That heavy bat with layers and layers of grips in the hands of this big man, coupled with his huge backlift, packed unbelievable power in his shots. When Clive Lloyd was firing on all cylinders he did not need much support at the other end. That was obvious here.

Collis King and 'King' Richards clinch the final

Lord's, June 23, 1979

Collis King

Hardly ever was Vivian Richards put in the shade by a mere mortal, and that too when he himself played a characteristically cavalier knock. But the big occasion seemed to have inspired young Collis King, who brought the house down with an exhilarating innings. King joined Richards with the West Indies in trouble at 99 for four in the 30th over. By lunch they had already taken the score to 125 off 34 overs. Richards was on 55 and King rapidly unbeaten on 19. After the break they went berserk, aided by the fact that the main bowlers were out of the attack. They launched a furious assault on the English, taking 38 runs off 6 overs from Geoff Boycott, and 27 off 4 from Graham Gooch. Wayne Larkins was carted around for 21 in 2 overs, making it a total of 86 runs in 12 overs. King holed out in the 51st over for a blazing 86 off just 66 balls with 10 fours and 3 sixes. The superb partnership realised 139 runs in only 21 overs. Richards then went into overdrive, hitting 43 out of 48 runs in the last 9 overs. He capped the amazing performance by lofting the last ball for a massive six. Richards was unbeaten with 138 off 157 deliveries, having hit 11 fours and 3 sixes as the West Indies accumulated 286 for nine. That was enough to retain the Prudential Cup.

Best World Cup analysis by Winston Davis

Leeds, June 11 &12, 1983

Winston Davis

Winston Davis did not get his share of glory because he happened to play at a time when great West Indies fast bowlers seemed to arrive as if by magic. But here in rainy Leeds he left an indelible mark on the foremost Limited-overs tournament. The wicket afforded generous lateral movement as the sun reappeared on the second day, and that suited the pace quartet. Graeme Wood received a nasty crack on the jaw by a Michael Holding snorter but the Aussies seemed to be progressing well. Davis had conceded 37 runs off 5 overs, having dismissed skipper Kim Hughes. But he soon got into the act. He removed the well-set David Hookes and Graham Yallop in his 6th over. Thereafter he scythed through the rest of the line-up. In a matter of just five-and-a-half overs he grabbed 6 wickets for 14 runs to bundle out Australia for 151. Davis' final figures read 7 for 51 off 10.3 overs. This was the best analysis in the World Cup and the only instance of a bowler claiming 7 wickets in a match until Glenn McGrath and Andy Bichel bagged 7 for 15 and 7 for 20 respectively 20 years later. It was a trail-blazing performance by the lean and wiry Davis.

David Houghton rattles Aussies

Southampton, June 16, 1983

David Houghton

Zimbabwe had already shocked Australia in their first match. Here in their return encounter, the canny hitter David Houghton had the Aussies on tenterhooks again. He attacked their bowling with gusto and nearly snatched an unlikely second successive win. Just when Zimbabwe seemed to be tottering, Houghton put on 103 for the 6th wicket with Kevin Curran in only 17 overs. Houghton was brilliant, bringing up a half-century in consecutive matches, and carrying on to play brilliant shots all round the wicket. He took 8 runs off a Rodney Hogg over as the paceman returned for a new spell. Trevor Chappell was the next to be given the treatment as Houghton swung one over square-leg for six. The asking-rate was now about 7.5 runs per over but Houghton was in his eighties and looking set to carry his side to their target of 273. It was then that Chappell and Hogg struck. A collapse ensued. Curran left for 35, and Houghton was pouched by Kim Hughes for a tremendous 84 off 108 balls, scored against the odds. He had jolted the Australians, and had he stayed for a few more overs, he may well have clinched victory for the underdogs. Houghton was magnificent on this day.

De Mel bowls Sri Lanka to victory

Derby, June 18, 1983

Asantha de Mel

If ever a bowling performance won a One-day match, it was this one by Asantha de Mel. He was Sri Lanka's leading paceman at the time and put up sterling performances every now and then. On this day de Mel bowled brilliantly. He struck early, deceiving New Zealand's best batsman Glenn Turner into spooning a catch to Roy Dias. Immediately after, he got the other opener John Wright to edge the ball to wicketkeeper Guy de Alwis. Suddenly, the Kiwis were two down for just 8 runs. New Zealand were always struggling after such a disastrous start. They were already six down for barely a hundred when de Mel again struck three quick blows. He had Warren Lees snapped up by Arjuna Ranatunga. Thereafter he dismissed Richard Hadlee, caught by Ranjan Madugalle, and a run later got Lance Cairns to hole out to Dias. That left New Zealand down for the count at 116 for nine. Martin Snedden and Ewan Chatfield did put up stiff resistance but de Mel, with help from Rumesh Ratnayake and Somachandra de Silva, had ensured that the Kiwis would not set too tough a target. De Mel finished with five for 32 in his 12 overs, his second five-wicket haul in a row.

Kapil Dev plays one of the greatest innings

Tunbridge Wells, June 18, 1983

Kapil Dev

Even before the spectators settled in their seats, Zimbabwe had reduced India to 17 for five. Gavaskar, Srikkanth, Amarnath, Patil and Yash Pal were all gone. It seemed as if the minnows were about to create a sensational upset. Kapil Dev had played many attacking innings under adverse circumstances. Would the Indian skipper rise to the occasion again? Rise he did, and how! Launching a ferocious attack, the like of which is rarely seen, he quickly destroyed all illusions of an early Indian surrender. He added 60 for the sixth wicket with Roger Binny who made 22. Ravi Shastri fell soon and India still found themselves in trouble at 78 for seven. Kapil shifted another gear and smashed the ball all over the park. Madan Lal offered solid support, scoring 17 in a 62-run partnership. When he left, the score was 140 for eight. Syed Kirmani joined Kapil, who now went into overdrive. They put on 126 in the final stretch, Kirmani's share being 24 not out. Kapil Dev had played an unforgettable hand, hitting an unbeaten 175, a World Cup record at that point. He batted for just three hours, facing only 138 balls and smashing 16 fours and 6 sixes - exactly 100 in boundaries. Truly a stunning innings.

Vivian Richards breaks record with ferocious knock

Karachi, October 13, 1987

Vivian Richards

Vivian Richards was one of the greatest batsmen in history. The Caribbean blaster was also an awesome striker of the ball, as we saw here. Often great innings like this come when the team is in strife. Richards walked in with Ravi Ratnayeke on a hat-trick. He settled down soon and then went on the rampage, stroking the ball freely in arrogant fashion, almost. Opener Desmond Haynes kept him company in a huge partnership of 182, then a record for the third wicket. The Sri Lankan attack came in for severe caning as the two experienced batsmen attacked with gusto. Haynes left after getting a hundred, but Richards carried on. By now he was unstoppable, playing shots only a genius like him could. Gus Logie lent able support and in next to no time, 58 minutes in fact, they had put on 116 runs. That amounted to two-runs-a-minute, unbelievable by conventional standards. By the time Richards was caught brilliantly by Roshan Mahanama, he had hit 181 off just 125 balls. On the way he smashed 16 fours and 7 sixes, and passed Kapil Dev's record score of 175 set four years earlier. It was Vivian Richards at his very best.

Geoff Marsh carries bat

Geoff Marsh

Chandigarh, October 27, 1987

Even in One-day cricket, carrying one's bat through an innings is a commendable feat. Sunil Gavaskar had done it in bizarre fashion against England the day the World Cup began in 1975, managing to score just 36 in 60 overs. The other instance was Glenn Turner's 171 not out, also in 60 overs against lowly-rated East Africa the same day. And so after 12 years came this resilient knock by Geoff Marsh, and in all 12 batsmen have carried their bats till the 2007 event. In 1987 the World Cup travelled away from England for the first time, and due to shorter hours of daylight in the sub-continental winters, the innings were curtailed to 50 overs. That was later to become the norm. Marsh was associated in a brilliant second-wicket partnership with Dean Jones. They put on 126 in 26 overs, annihilating the New Zealand attack. Marsh batted serenely as wickets fell all around him. In fact, had he cast his wicket away, Australia may well have been shot out for a meagre score. He returned unbeaten with 126 off 149 balls, out of a total of 251 at the end of 50 overs. In all Marsh hit 12 fours and 3 sixes, a sterling performance that took the match away from the Antipodean neighbours.

A hat-trick for Chetan Sharma

Nagpur, October 31, 1987

Chetan Sharma

A hat-trick is always cause for much jubilation. But when an excitable character like Chetan Sharma achieves the feat in a World Cup match on home soil, you can imagine the frenzy on the field and in the stands. New Zealand were progressing well, having put up 181 runs for the loss of four wickets. Just then Ravi Shastri dismissed the well-set Dipak Patel for 40. A run later the drama began to unfold. Delivering the fourth ball of his 6th over, Chetan Sharma clean bowled Ken Rutherford, who had played a dogged innings. Next ball he again went through the defence of Ian Smith for another bull's eye. There was now a huge buzz around the stadium. Skipper Kapil Dev set an attacking field to help the little paceman achieve the coveted feat of three-in-a-row. He need not have bothered as Sharma pitched right in the block-hole, Ewan Chatfield missed, and the ball crashed into the stumps. There was pandemonium as the ecstatic bowler lay on his back amid a deafening roar. This was the first hat-trick in the World Cup. Saqlain Mushtaq achieved the feat in 1999, followed by Chaminda Vaas and Brett Lee in 2003, and Lasith Malinga with four wickets in four balls in 2007. This match also saw a maiden One-day century by the legendary Sunil Gavaskar, and that too off just 85 deliveries with 10 fours and 3 sixes.

Graham Gooch sweeps England into final

Graham Gooch

Bombay, November 5, 1987

Reigning champions India were firm favourites to make it to the final on home ground. But they had not reckoned with the English fetish for strategy. Anticipating that a turning wicket would be prepared to suit Maninder Singh and Ravi Shastri, they devised a plan whereby Graham Gooch would sweep anything even remotely pitched up by the two left-arm spinners. It worked. The Indians were perplexed by this audacity of repeatedly hitting against the spin. They could not decide on the line they should bowl under the circumstances, and kept feeding Gooch who played the shot with abandon. Skipper Kapil Dev must have been hoping that such bravado would not last too long. But he was wrong. Gooch kept swiping from even outside the off-stump. A 117-run third-wicket stand with skipper Mike Gatting laid a solid foundation. By the time Gooch eventually holed out to Krish Srikkanth off Maninder, the Indian dream seemed to have vanished. Gooch had hit 115 off 136 deliveries with 11 boundaries. England finished on 254 for six off 50 overs. On this slow, turning track it was enough to carry the day. India had been outsmarted by the English think-tank, and defeated by a savvy Gooch.

Star Turns

Martin Crowe hammers
blistering half-century

Martin Crowe

Napier, March 3, 1992

It was a match badly affected by rain. The New Zealand innings was interrupted twice, and their batting quota was restricted to just 20.5 overs. They had to do something fast, and in the process Zimbabwe took two quick wickets. But that only set the stage for skipper Martin Crowe to get together with Andrew Jones in a 129-run stand. Jones got a half-century, but it was the majestic Crowe who stole the show. He brought cheer to this dismal, wet day and provided glimpses of the masterly batsman that he undoubtedly was. His exquisite strokeplay warmed the hearts of all who were fortunate enough to watch. He cracked a fifty in a mere 30 deliveries, equalling the World Cup record then held by Chris Old and Imran Khan. By 2007, Brendon McCullum brought the mark down to 20 balls. When rain finally halted the Kiwi innings, Crowe had hit a classy unbeaten 74 off just 44 balls. It is innings like this that set batsmen like Martin Crowe apart. They have such a wide range of shots that they need not resort to crude methods to boost the tempo of scoring. Crowe's heroics meant that New Zealand posted a score of 162 at nearly 8-runs-an-over. That was far too much for Zimbabwe.

Inspired spell by Meyrick Pringle

Meyrick Pringle

Christchurch, March 5, 1992

As South Africa emerged from their cocoon and re-entered the international arena after a lapse of 21 years, many felt that they would take some time to get their bearings at the top level. But the gritty men from the land of Pollock and Procter surprised everyone. They settled down quickly and put up a splendid show in the 1992 World Cup. Reflecting their positive attitude was the lanky paceman Meyrick Pringle. His team was able to muster just 200 for eight in 50 overs against the West Indies, now beginning to decline. Pringle struck early as the rising star Brian Lara slashed and was snapped up by Jonty Rhodes, a man already drawing rave comments for his fielding brilliance. Not long after, he sent back the captain, Richie Richardson, leg-before-wicket. Pringle then had Carl Hooper caught by Kepler Wessels for a duck. A similar calamity befell Keith Arthurton. The West Indies found themselves precariously placed at 19 for four. They did not recover sufficiently from this sorry state. Meyrick Pringle's final analysis was 8-4-11-4, simply amazing and one of the best in the World Cup. He helped his side clinch not only the match, but also a berth in the semi-finals.

Botham displays his class at last

Ian Botham

Sydney (D/N), March 5, 1992

Ian Botham was one of the greatest allrounders the game has seen. But for some inexplicable reason his showing in the World Cup was not at par with his prowess. He played in 1979 and 1983 without assuming a lead role. Returning for the 1992 edition, he was past his prime even though he had been pitch-forked into the role of opening batsman. But it was as a bowler, and a second change bowler at that, that Botham first shone in this match. He bowled Australian skipper Allan Border, another great who did not have much to show for his efforts in the World Cup. In his next over it was Botham of yore. He got Ian Healy to hole out to Neil Fairbrother, and then had Peter Taylor leg-before and Craig McDermott snapped up by Philip DeFreitas, both without scoring. Botham had grabbed three wickets in an over, and four in 7 balls. This was the Botham magic that everyone had known over the past decade-and-a-half. The burly allrounder had not finished yet. He gave a flying start to the England innings, raising 107 runs with skipper Graham Gooch. Botham slammed 53 runs off 77 balls with 6 fours to set up an easy win over the traditional rivals. 'Guy the Gorilla' had redeemed his reputation.

Greatbatch and Martin Crowe stun West Indies

Mark Greatbatch

Auckland, March 8, 1992

How many times did Mark Greatbatch and Martin Crowe dazzle in the 1992 World Cup? They were in superb form, and while Greatbatch improvised by hitting over the top in the early overs, Crowe batted with customary brilliance. As Greatbatch waded into the West Indies pace attack, still a potent force, the man at the other end Rod Latham looked on in admiration for the most part. The latter's share in the opening stand of 67 was just 14. Greatbatch raced to his half-century, hitting 6 fours and 3 sixes, a total of 42 runs in boundaries. His first 22 runs comprised just boundaries - 4 fours and a six. He fell for 63 off 77 deliveries, having crashed 7 fours and 3 sixes. Martin Crowe slipped into his seat, and once again batted like a champion. He scored 81 of the finest at a-run-a-ball with 12 fours. He returned unbeaten, having guided his team to a memorable win over the once-mighty West Indies. It was another chapter in the Kiwi run of successes in the tournament. This was in the main due to the batting of Martin Crowe and Mark Greatbatch, and again they had belted the attack to the delight of the home fans.

Inzamam - new hero in the making

Auckland, March 21, 1992

Inzamam-ul-Haq

New Zealand had won their first seven matches in the 1992 World Cup. For Pakistan it had so far been a lacklustre tournament. The two met in their last engagement and Pakistan won, thereby managing to squeak through to the semi-finals. As it happened, they clashed again in the penultimate round. New Zealand put up an imposing 262 for seven in 50 overs. Pakistan seemed to be faltering at 140 for four as the young Inzamam-ul-Haq joined veteran Javed Miandad. Calm, deadpan Inzamam began playing with remarkable maturity. He was soon rattling the fence repeatedly. He reached his half-century in a mere 31 balls, taking just one delivery more than the then World Cup record. It seemed that the talented youngster would win the match on his own. Even the belligerent Miandad was forced to play second fiddle. As Pakistan began to canter home, Inzamam was run out, but by then he had carried his team to within striking distance of a thrilling win. He scored 60 off just 37 deliveries, making 7 hits to the fence and one over it. His partnership with Miandad was worth 87 runs, and it ensured that Pakistan would reach their first World Cup final.

Wasim Akram
strikes crucial blows

Melbourne (D/N), March 25, 1992

Wasim Akram

It was the first final in coloured clothing and under lights, and the setting in the massive, fully packed MCG was more akin to a big football match. Pakistan made an uncertain start before the senior pros Imran Khan and Javed Miandad put up a century partnership. But the scoring-rate needed a boost, and both were dismissed trying to force the pace. It was then that Wasim Akram joined Inzamam-ul-Haq. They took the attack by the scruff of the neck in their bid to raise a winning score. Inzamam smashed 42 off 35 deliveries, but the left-handed Akram brought the crowd to its feet. He thrashed the ball all around, hitting up 33 off just 19 deliveries, and helping Pakistan reach 249 for six in 50 overs. Akram was soon back in action with the ball. Right away he had Ian Botham caught behind for a blob. Later, just as Neil Fairbrother and Allan Lamb were making a match of it, Akram struck like a deadly cobra. He clean bowled Lamb, and created a sensation off the very next ball by also shattering the stumps of Chris Lewis. The English back had been broken, and the jubilant Pakistanis went on to lift the glittering crystal globe. Wasim Akram was the undisputed star on the big day.

Star Turns

Mumbaikars' dream soured by Mark and Damien

Mumbai (D/N), February 27, 1996

Mark Waugh

When Sachin Tendulkar bats on his home ground, and scores as many as 90 masterly runs, the Mumbaikars' day is made. Not on this occasion. Mark Waugh was in tremendous form in this tournament, hitting an unprecedented three centuries. He notched one of them here. Damien Fleming also made his mark with his accurate medium-pace which skidded through to surprise the batsmen. Together they caused mayhem in the Indian ranks. Mark Waugh was at his fluent best, timing the ball sweetly and making batting look so easy. He put on 103 for the first wicket with skipper Mark Taylor. Even in attack Mark Waugh was elegant. He tonked Venkatapathy Raju for sixes over mid-wicket and then straight back, and pulled Javagal Srinath for another mighty six before being run out for 126 off just 135 balls. Fleming took over thereafter. With India on 7, he trapped Ajay Jadeja leg-before, and then clean bowled Vinod Kambli. Later he had skipper Mohammad Azharuddin playing on to his stumps. Finally, he returned to bowl Anil Kumble and have Srinath caught by Shane Lee. Fleming bagged five for 36 off 9 overs to clinch a fine win for Australia.

Richie Richardson
at his best

Jaipur, March 4, 1996

Richie Richardson

It was, for the most part, not a happy tournament for skipper Richie Richardson. His team reached its nadir, being upset by Kenya. It also marked the end of his international career. But Richardson had his moments. The biggest was in this encounter which was crucial if the West Indies were to make it to the quarter-finals. Australia had scored 229 for six in 50 overs. Richardson joined Brian Lara after the early loss of the openers. The two maestros were in fine form, putting on 87 in just 17.4 overs. Once Lara left, it was Richardson all the way. He played a true captain's knock. Shivnaraine Chanderpaul, Roger Harper and Jimmy Adams gave fine support as Richardson went after the bowling. He was a man determined to redeem the sagging reputation of the West Indies. The Australians, hard as they tried, could not dislodge him. He carried his team to victory, and into the knock-out stage. His superb unbeaten 93 off 133 deliveries contained 10 fours and a six. Like a true champion, Richardson hit out at his critics with a sterling performance at the wicket. He led the West Indies into the semi-final after 13 years, where he played another fine knock as he was left to fight a losing battle.

The Jayasuriya carnival carries on

Faisalabad, March 9, 1996

Sanath Jayasuriya

There are some players who hang around the international scene playing a minor role, and then suddenly take off at some stage to become star performers. Sanath Jayasuriya is one such. For some years he bowled slow left-arm and batted down the order without being noticed. But once he was asked to open, the Lankan became a different player, hammering the new ball in the manner of some of the fiercest hitters in history. The 1996 tournament saw him play a few scintillating innings like the one in the quarter-final against England at Faisalabad. Jayasuriya made the idea of a spinner, Richard Illingworth, opening the bowling look a stupid one. He tonked four consecutive fours off the slow bowler, and hit three more boundaries in a Darren Gough over. It was Philip Defreitas' turn next. Jayasuriya hit him for a six and a four in his first over, and 2 fours and 2 sixes, besides a two in his second - a total of 32 runs off DeFreitas in two overs. Jayasuriya seemed to be on course to break Clive Lloyd's record for the fastest World Cup century in 82 deliveries. But he was stumped for 82 off only 44 balls with 13 fours and 3 sixes in 67 minutes. It was an awesome display indeed.

South Africans undone by Lara

Karachi, March 11, 1996

Brian Lara

The South Africans had an unbeaten run in the league phase; the West Indies had nearly been knocked out. But when it came to the quarter-final clash, the brilliance of one man turned the tide and the fancied team bit the dust. Such was the genius of Brian Lara that he could skim against the tide and carve out unlikely wins when least expected. The openers had given a flying start and Lara capitalised on it fully. Treating pacemen and spinners alike, he reached his half-century off only 45 balls. Once there, he meted out rough treatment to veteran off-spinner Pat Symcox, hammering five boundaries in one over, four of them in succession. Lara raised 138 for the second wicket in less than 25 overs along with Shivnaraine Chanderpaul. The West Indies were now 180 for two in just 30.5 overs. Lara blazed on, bringing up his first century in the World Cup off just 83 balls, one delivery outside Clive Lloyd's record. He went on to score 111 off only 94 deliveries with 16 fours. Even though the West Indies faded somewhat after his departure, Lara had ensured that they would post a total large enough for the bowlers to end the Proteas' ten-match winning spree.

The Cup is Sri Lanka's thanks to Aravinda

Lahore (D/N), March 17, 1996

Aravinda de Silva

The 'Mad Max' of yesteryear had matured into one of the finest strokeplayers of the present. He had played a superb innings in the semi-final against India, and now the inspired Sri Lankan team was on the threshold of a world title. Aravinda de Silva was the man they were looking up to again. Australia had raised a formidable score of 241 for seven, de Silva capturing three wickets for 42 with his off-spin. Sanath Jayasuriya and Romesh Kaluwitharana were again dismissed cheaply, and it was 23 for two as de Silva joined Asanka Gurusinha. From then on it was de Silva all the way. He was dominant and technically proficient, driving, cutting and pulling in a manner that rendered the Australians helpless. His half-century came at a-run-a-ball. The third-wicket partnership realised 125 runs off 25 overs, but Gurusinha's exit saw the vastly experienced skipper Ranatunga join the beautifully set de Silva. They were determined to win the big prize as de Silva raised his century in 119 balls. The honour of bringing up the title-winning runs was de Silva's. His unbeaten 107 with 13 fours came off 124 balls. Sri Lanka's day of glory was synonymous with a huge high in the career of Aravinda de Silva.

Rare double by 'keeper Jacobs

Southampton, May 24, 1999

Ridley Jacobs

It is not often that a wicketkeeper steals the show. On this day West Indian Ridley Jacobs was the star. Having already established a reputation as a resolute fighter, Jacobs showed that he could be a match-winner too. As the pacemen exploited the helpful conditions, the New Zealand slide began with Jacobs snapping up Nathan Astle off Curtly Ambrose with just two runs on the board. He was in the frame right through, pouching a snick from skipper Stephen Fleming. He had a hand, or glove, in the dismissals of the well-set Craig McMillan and Adam Parore. Finally, Jacobs caught Gavin Larsen to equal the World Cup record of five dismissals in an innings jointly held by Syed Kirmani, Jimmy Adams, Rashid Latif and Nayan Mongia. Adam Gilchrist took 6 catches against Namibia in 2003, surpassing this feat. Left-handed Jacobs then opened the West Indies innings with Sherwin Campbell, and saw his side to victory, returning with an unbeaten 80 in a score of 158 for three off 44.2 overs. He faced 131 balls, hitting 8 fours and a six in his second half-century of the tournament. It was one of the most sterling displays by a wicketkeeper in the World Cup, reminiscent of compatriot Deryck Murray's heroics against Pakistan in 1975.

Dravid, Ganguly revel in an awesome partnership

Sourav Ganguly

Taunton, May 26, 1999

Reigning champions Sri Lanka's cup of misery was full when Rahul Dravid and Sourav Ganguly treated their attack with disdain, nay contempt. The Indian pair hoisted the highest-ever partnership, by far, not only in the World Cup but in all One-day Internationals. Dravid, coming in one-down, was first off the mark with his brilliant strokeplay. Opener Ganguly cut loose later, hitting a flurry of sixes. Records tumbled one after another as they piled on the runs. For the first time a 300-run partnership was put up in a One-day International. They were separated only after putting on 318 runs. Ganguly's 7 sixes equalled Vivian Richards' World Cup record, and Sachin Tendulkar's Indian record in all One-day Internationals. Ricky Ponting hit 8 sixes in the 2003 final to go one better, with Imran Nazir and Adam Gilchrist emulating the feat in 2007. Dravid became the second batsman, after Mark Waugh, to score back-to-back hundreds in the World Cup. Ganguly hit up 183, India's highest in One-day Internationals then. It was the second-highest ever in the World Cup after South African Gary Kirsten's 188 not out against UAE in 1996, and fourth in the all-time One day list behind Saeed Anwar's 194 and Vivian Richards' 189. Sachin Tendulkar scored the finest double century in 2010.

Allrounder Johnson's heroics upset favourites

Chelmsford, May 29, 1999

Neil Johnson

Neil Johnson came into his own in the 1999 World Cup. He was one of the stars in a Zimbabwe side that caused a few surprises. Perhaps the biggest was the upset of joint favourites, South Africa, and this ensured Zimbabwe a berth in the super-six. Johnson opened as usual with Grant Flower, and the two put on 65. The momentum was kept up as the southpaw added another 66 with Murray Goodwin. Johnson batted freely, driving and pulling with assurance. When he was caught by Shaun Pollock off Allan Donald for 76, Zimbabwe were well on course for a fighting total. Johnson was soon back in action with the glossy white ball in his hand. Off the very first delivery of the innings he had the hapless Gary Kirsten caught by Andy Whittal. The slide had begun. Two more wickets tumbled soon, after which Johnson struck a huge blow by having the in-form Jacques Kallis caught behind for a duck. Bowling unchanged in his eight-over spell, Johnson then yorked skipper Hansie Cronje. The Cup aspirants were gasping at 34 for five. They did recover somewhat through Shaun Pollock and Lance Klusener, but it was too late. Man-of-the-match Neil Johnson had already pulled the rug from under them.

McGrath rises to the occasion

Glenn McGrath

Manchester, May 30, 1999

A win in this match was essential for Australia to make it to the super-six. It is at times such as this that class tells. Someone had to pull off something special, and it was Glenn McGrath's turn to show that he ranked among the greats. He exploited the seaming Old Trafford track to deadly effect, leaving the old rivals for cricketing supremacy battered and beaten, and ejected from the showpiece event. As always, bowling from as close to the stumps as anyone has ever done, McGrath had the West Indies in strife right from the start. He had Sherwin Campbell caught by Mark Waugh for 2, and then trapped Jimmy Adams for a duck using his wicket-to-wicket bowling to deadly effect. It was 7 for two, and not long after he had Brian Lara comprehensively beaten and bowled. Despite Ridley Jacobs' grit while carrying his bat for an unbeaten 49, the West Indies failed to recover. McGrath returned to dismiss Mervyn Dillon and Courtney Walsh, finishing with five for 14, the best figures in the tournament. A target of 111 was hardly enough to test the resolute Aussies and they romped home with plenty of wickets and overs to spare. They had to be grateful to McGrath for this.

Saqlain bags World Cup's second hat-trick

Kennington Oval, London, June 11, 1999

Saqlain Mushtaq

The sheer rarity of a hat-trick makes it a memorable event. Only once had this three-in-a-row strike been achieved in the World Cup by Indian medium-pacer Chetan Sharma against New Zealand in 1987. Here, Zimbabwe were sliding to an ignominious defeat at 123 for seven after 40 overs, chasing an improbable target of 272. Like Sunil Gavaskar in 1987, the brilliant opener Saeed Anwar cracked a match-winning 103 now. The pressure was solely on Zimbabwe. But a hat-trick is a hat-trick, no matter what the conditions or who the opponents. You may take two-in-a-row but when it comes to that vital third, you need immense concentration, great skill and a very steady hand. First, Saqlain Mushtaq had Henry Olonga perplexed and stumped by Moin Khan. He handed out the same prescription next ball to Adam Huckle. Finally, Mpumelelo Mbangwa could not figure out what trick the master off-spinner was up to. Deceived as the ball dipped in flight, and unsure whether it would turn in or go away with the arm, the tailenders had no answer to Saqlain's wiles. His hat-trick was the icing on the cake for Pakistan. Chaminda Vaas and Brett Lee emulated the feat in 2003, and Lasith Malinga grabbed four in four in 2007.

Star Turns

Jayasuriya and Styris fire in contrasting scenarios

Bloemfontein, February 10, 2003

Scott Styris

A slow wicket and tight New Zealand bowling kept Sanath Jayasuriya in check. He settled into a long second-wicket stand with Hashan Tillekeratne. Jayasuriya was unstoppable once he reached his fifty. He played thundering cuts and pulls, not hesitating to loft the ball. He slammed Andre Adams for three fours through the covers in the same over. Jayasuriya brought up his 16th hundred in 288 One-dayers, the first in his four World Cups, in one of which he was player-of-the-tournament. He carried on relentless. His side was in a position of dominance by the time he was out for 120 off 125 balls with 14 boundaries. The 170-run partnership was Sri Lanka's best for the second wicket in the World Cup. They totalled 272 for seven. Kiwis had lost two wickets for 2 runs when Scott Styris came in. Wickets tumbled and the asking-rate climbed despite spirited stands with Chris Cairns and Chris Harris. Styris played the innings of his life, battling to his maiden hundred in 52 One-dayers. He launched a blitzkrieg, slamming 6 sixes and 3 fours. He was last out for 141 off just 125 balls, with his team miles away from the target.

Symonds storm

Andrew Symonds

Johannesburg, February 11, 2003

Australia made an inauspicious start to their title-defence, first losing Shane Warne to a failed drug test, and then sent reeling at 86 for four by the Pakistani pacemen. Robust Queenslander Andrew Symonds helped skipper Ricky Ponting add 60. Symonds was renowned for his big hitting but made little impact at the international level. He chose this stage to show that he had arrived. Reaching his half-century off 60 balls, and with the lower-order for company, he tore the attack to shreds. He put on 70 off 9.2 overs with Brad Hogg, and 54 off 6.4 overs with Ian Harvey. Symonds' second fifty came off only 32 balls. It was his first century in 55 One-day Internationals. He slammed 19 runs off nine balls from Wasim Akram, including a straight six. He went on to slam an unbeaten 143 off just 125 balls with 18 fours and 2 sixes. It was the highest score by an Australian in the World Cup till Matthew Hayden bettered it in 2007. Australia piled up 310 for eight. The dispirited Pakistanis folded up for 228. Symonds capped a magnificent performance with a blinder of a catch at mid-wicket to dismiss Yousuf Youhana, now known as Mohammad Yousuf. This was Symonds' day.

Vaas foursome

Chaminda Vaas

Pietermaritzburg, February 14, 2003

Chaminda Vaas was prone to dazzle periodically. He took a record One-day haul of eight for 19, inclusive of a hat-trick, against Zimbabwe a season earlier. On a slightly damp pitch here at Pietermaritzburg, Vaas created a flutter with his first ball. He bowled Hannan Sarkar through the gate as the Bangladesh opener tried to drive an in-swinger. Next ball, Mohammad Ashraful lobbed a catch back to Vaas. Could there be a hat-trick off the first three balls of the match? Ehsanul Haque fished as the ball slanted across him. It flicked the outside edge and flew to Mahela Jayawardene at second slip. It was an incredible hat-trick, unprecedented for the opening over of a match, and third hat-trick in the World Cup after Chetan Sharma in 1987 and Saqlain Mushtaq in 1999. Sanwar Hossain cover-drove the fourth ball for a four. Vaas bowled a wide, and straightened the fifth to find Sanwar plumb in front. The score was 5 for four. A dot ball ended the sensational over. Opener Mohammad Al Shariar was Vaas' fifth victim. Vaas dismissed tailender Mashrafe Mortaza too. His six for 25 was now Sri Lanka's best in the World Cup. Compatriot Lasith Malinga grabbed four wickets in four balls in 2007.

World Cup's fastest century at Centurion by a John Davison

John Davison

Centurion, February 24, 2003

Canada's John Davison cracked the fastest World Cup century off 67 balls against the West Indies. A 32-year-old off-spinner playing first-class cricket for South Australia, Davison outpaced Clive Lloyd's century off 82 deliveries in the 1975 final. Davison hit up 111 off 76 deliveries with 6 sixes and 8 fours. None of his teammates scored 20 in a total of 202. While Davison was swinging his bat merrily, Ishwar Maraj contributed 16 to an opening stand of 96, and Desmond Chumney 19 to a partnership of 59. With a crowd of about 10,000 cheering the underdogs, Davison brought up his thunderous hundred with a mighty six over long-on off Mervyn Dillon. Matthew Hayden set a new mark in 2007. Fortune did favour the brave Davison on this day as he was dropped on 55 and 76, and was nearly bowled on 71 as the ball failed to dislodge the bails. He was brilliantly caught by Vasbert Drakes on the long-on fence. Wavell Hinds smacked the fastest fifty in World Cup history off 24 balls. Lara soon bettered it by a delivery. There were quicker fifties in 2007. West Indies achieved the best-ever run-rate of 10.04 in One-dayers and recorded a runaway win by seven wickets, but the glory was all Davison's.

Nehra swings at night

Ashish Nehra

Durban (D/N), February 26, 2003

India scored a round 250. Then the frail 23-year-old left-armer Ashish Nehra astounded with his speed, touching almost 150 kph, and consistently bowling at 90 mph (144 kph), about as fast as Shane Bond, third quickest after Shoaib Akhtar and Brett Lee. Nehra bowled close to the stumps over-the-wicket, and kept the ball up around the off-stump. He seamed it away just a bit, or straightened it a trifle. The ball probably skidded a little extra at night. English batsmen had no clue. Coming on first-change after the openers had gone early, Nehra had skipper Nasser Hussain caught at the wicket. There was mayhem as he straightened the next ball, trapping Alec Stewart leg-before. The prolific Michael Vaughan nicked Nehra, Rahul Dravid grabbing his 50th catch as wicketkeeper. Paul Collingwood edged Nehra to Virender Sehwag at second slip. Soon Craig White tickled a Nehra delivery to Dravid. Finally, Nehra had Ronnie Irani taken at first slip by Sehwag. England were 107 for eight. The match was over bar the shouting. Nehra had taken six for 23 in his unchanged 10-over spell, best figures for India in the World Cup.

The power of Tendulkar

Sachin Tendulkar

Centurion, March 1, 2003

Pakistan, desperately needing a win, logged up 273 runs. Tendulkar stroked Wasim Akram's third ball through the covers. Virender Sehwag square-cut the last for another four. Then came the carnage. Shoaib Akhtar came on at the other end and Tendulkar slashed the fourth ball over backward point for a six. He whipped the next one to square-leg, and on-drove the last, for successive boundaries. Eighteen runs came off the over and Akhtar was promptly taken off. Tendulkar had established ascendency in two overs. The fifty came up in five overs. Sehwag and Sourav Ganguly got out to successive deliveries. But Tendulkar was in a different zone. He treated every bowler with disdain, hitting a dozen exquisite boundaries besides the six. Mohammad Kaif helped add 102. Tendulkar got cramps but refused a runner till he was almost immobile. A hobbling Tendulkar fended at a vicious Akhtar bouncer and was caught on the off-side for 98. He had faced just 75 balls and placed his team in a dominant position. India were 177 in the 28th over. Rahul Dravid and Yuvraj Singh ushered in victory. It was another page in the saga of Sachin Tendulkar.

Kloppenburg's double Dutch delight

Feiko Kloppenburg

Bloemfontein, March 3, 2003

Feiko Kloppenburg's versatility on a true Goodyear Park pitch helped replicate the ICC Champions Trophy 2001 final win. Kloppenburg put on 228 for the second wicket with Klaas-Jan van Noortwijk, Holland's best in One-dayers and third highest for the wicket in the World Cup. Kloppenburg became the first Netherlands batsman to score a One-day International century, reaching the mark off 127 balls. Van Noortwijk scored his hundred off 111 deliveries. Both got cramps under the hot sun. Kloppenburg fell for 121 off 142 balls with 6 fours and 4 sixes. Van Noortwijk hit an unbeaten 134, highest for the Dutch in One-dayers, off 129 deliveries with 11 fours and 3 sixes. The total of 314 for four was their highest in One-dayers, and by an associate member in the World Cup. Namibia sparkled and then faded. Seamer Kloppenburg had Jan Berry Burger caught, and bowled Daniel Keulder to end a fighting third-wicket stand. He removed Louis Burger and Gerrie Snyman in two balls, taking four for 42. Off-spinner Adeel Raja had the same figures. Kloppenburg was the first to hit a century and take four wickets in a World Cup match.

Just Bond-age, no Lee-way for batsmen

Shane Bond

Port Elizabeth, March 11, 2003

Shane Bond was again Australia's nemesis as Stephen Fleming inserted them on a moist pitch. Matthew Hayden nicked Bond to Brendon McCullum. Adam Gilchrist fired till Bond trapped him leg-before. Bond had harangued Ricky Ponting; again he dismissed him. Bond ended Damien Martyn's resistance, having him caught behind, and trapped Brad Hogg leg-before first ball. He bowled Ian Harvey, sending Australia reeling at 84 for seven. Bond's six for 23 was New Zealand's best in One-dayers. Brett Lee was hit for 31 runs in a five-over spell, but returned with a vengeance as the ball reversed. He forced top-scorer Fleming to top-edge to Gilchrist. A lethal yorker thudded into McCullum's pads, and a thunderbolt crashed into Jacob Oram's stumps first ball. Lee was on a hat-trick in the next over but was denied by Andre Adams. Next ball, he castled the batsman, his third wicket in four balls. He ended with a theatrical return catch off Bond's bat. Lee snared five for 11 in a second spell of 4.1 overs, his first five-wicket haul in the World Cup. New Zealand lost by 96 runs. Bond was man-of-the-match for rocking the champions.

Lee takes hat-trick, Karim tricks yellow hats

Asif Karim

Durban (D/N), March 15, 2003

Brett Lee struck thrice in a row. But 39-year-old left-arm spinner Asif Karim waylaid the Australians on this Durban night. Lee's tenth delivery crunched into Kennedy Otieno's elbow, then dislodged the bails. Otieno was helped off in excruciating pain. Brijal Patel bagged a golden duck, hanging out his bat for Ricky Ponting to snap him up. Otieno's brother, David Obuya, was in a nerve-wracking situation. Lee fired an in-swinging yorker that clattered into the stumps. Kenya tottered at 3 for three in 4 overs. A middle-order revival took Kenya to 174 for eight. Lee had analysis of 8-3-14-3. Australia made a rousing start but Karim turned the game. Kenya's 1999 World Cup captain, now recalled, spun a web. He trapped Ponting leg-before, had Darren Lehmann pouched by 'keeper David Obuya, and caught Brad Hogg off his own bowling. Karim had grabbed three wickets for none in two overs. Australia lurched at 117 for five. As Andrew Symonds and Ian Harvey scored at the other end, Karim conceded three runs in 49 deliveries before being hit for the winning boundary. His stint of 8.2-6-7-3 won him his first man-of-the-match award.

Ponting's hour of triumph

Ricky Ponting

Johannesburg, March 23, 2003

The Australians won all their eleven matches in the tournament. Skipper Ricky Ponting wrested the title with a contemptuous hundred. Sourav Ganguly won the toss in rain-swept Johannesburg and put Australia in, but his bowlers sprayed the ball and runs came in a torrent. Adam Gilchrist and Matthew Hayden brought up the hundred before the 15th over was up. Ponting strode in at 105, Damien Martyn joined him at 125. From then on, the match went only one way. Martyn set the pace, reaching his fifty off 46 balls; Ponting took 74 deliveries. Then the captain accelerated, and eventually seized full control. The Indians fed him on the on-side. Ponting had to make only a couple of straight hits, hardly any on the off, and made merry on the leg-side. He raced to his 13th One-day hundred in 103 balls, dealing mainly in sixes, bludgeoning eight, the most in a World Cup match, besides 4 fours. Imran Nazir and Adam Gilchrist also struck 8 sixes in an innings in 2007. The last 15 overs produced 143 runs, the unbroken partnership tallied 234, and the total soared to 359. The jubilant captain returned with 140 in his kitty, off just 121 deliveries. He had batted India out.

Herschelle Gibbs
maximises over

Herschelle Gibbs)

Basseterre, March 16, 2007

The peerless Gary Sobers smashed 6 sixes in an over after about a hundred years of first-class cricket. The unlikely Ravi Shastri replicated the feat. Herschelle Gibbs became the first to achieve it in One-day Internationals after 36 years. Twenty20 saw this accomplishment quickly when Yuvraj Singh tonked 6-in-6 in the inaugural Twenty20 World Championship six months later. Gibbs revelled in the picnic with minnows Holland, cruising on 32 off 30 deliveries with 3 fours and a six off Luuk van Troost. Leg-spinner Daan van Bunge bowled the 30th over. Gibbs stepped out, lofting the first ball over long-on. The next was flighted and drifting towards leg-and-middle, and Gibbs smote it atop long-off. The third was flat; Gibbs nonchalantly struck it again over long-off. Van Bunge aimed for the block-hole too, but it turned into a low full toss which Gibbs flat-batted above mid-wicket. For variety, van Bunge slipped a short ball outside off, but Gibbs bludgeoned it off the back-foot wide of long-off. There was an air of expectancy. The sixth delivery was outside off-stump again but full; Gibbs blasted it over mid-wicket. Johnnie Walker donated $1 million as promised to the Habitat for Humanity charity, which campaigns against poverty the world over. Gibbs' 7 sixes came off 8 balls. He hit 72 off 40 deliveries, cracking four boundaries besides.

Hayden blasts fastest ton

Basseterre, March 24, 2007

Matthew Hayden

Conditions were perfect, a flat batting track and short boundaries. Matthew Hayden bludgeoned the South African bowlers, racing to the fastest century in the World Cup off a mere 66 deliveries, one less than Canadian John Davison's feat in 2003. Hayden and Adam Gilchrist raised 106 in 14.5 overs. Hayden straight-drove his first ball to the boundary. He later square-cut Shaun Pollock again fiercely to the boundary, then smote him for two sixes in the same over. His fifty came in just 37 balls. Hayden glanced Andrew Hall to the fine-leg boundary and blasted the next over long-off for a six. He rocketed 3 fours in a Charl Langeveldt over. He was on 94 off 65 balls as Graeme Smith floated in his off-spinner. Hayden smashed it straight to claim the coveted record. He was dismissed in the next over, having delighted the crowd with his 101 off 68 deliveries, rocketing 14 fours and 4 sixes. Ricky Ponting and Michael Clarke scored quickfire nineties, adding 161 in 130 balls. Australia posted their highest World Cup total of 377 for six. Smith and Abraham de Villiers hoisted 160 runs in 21 overs for South Africa. De Villiers smashed 92 in 70 deliveries but South Africa hurtled downhill, losing by 83 runs. Hayden's fierce power hitting won the day.

Super Hayden hoists highest Aussie score

Matthew Hayden

North Sound, March 27-28, 2007

After being dropped from the Australian One-day side, Matthew Hayden hit up his country's highest score in this format only five weeks earlier, an unbeaten 181 against New Zealand at Hamilton. Then in the previous match he smashed the fastest hundred in the World Cup off the South Africans. Now he blazed to Australia's highest score in the World Cup too, surpassing Andrew Symonds' unbeaten 143 against Pakistan in 2003. On the virgin track of the Sir Vivian Richards Stadium, Hayden hit his first boundary off the 21st ball that he faced, rocketing Jerome Taylor through extra-cover, but he hit the next one too in the same direction for another four. He accelerated after the 20th over. His partnership with Michael Clarke realised 98 runs. Hayden struck his first six off Marlon Samuels. He brought up his hundred off 110 deliveries, then struck two consecutive boundaries off Darren Powell. Hayden slammed Taylor over long-on for a six, then a boundary through extra-cover, and a huge one straight into the stands, off consecutive deliveries. In the next over he smashed Samuels for two off-side boundaries, then a six over mid-wicket. He smashed 158 off 143 deliveries with 14 fours and 4 sixes. None of his team-mates got to fifty. Australia finished with 322 for six. West Indies were never in the hunt. Australia triumphed by 103 runs.

Irrepressible Jayasuriya's versatile act

Providence, April 1, 2007

Sanath Jayasuriya

Sanath Jayasuriya brought back memories of 1996 as his willow blazed again. Then his left round arm delivered the knockout punch at the hosts. He equalled Sachin Tendulkar's record of 384 One-day Internationals and also took the second spot in career run-aggregate behind the Indian maestro. Jayasuriya glided left-arm seamer Ian Bradshaw to the boundary, and slammed the next atop mid-off for another four. Medium-pacer Dwayne Smith was struck for a four above cover, a straight six, a slower one swept to the fence behind square, and a drive off the back-foot through the covers, 18 runs in all. Ten came off the next over by Chris Gayle, nine to Jayasuriya. He raised his 63rd fifty off 47 deliveries, then pulled Jerome Taylor over mid-wicket for a six. This was his 233rd six in One-dayers, beating Shahid Afridi's mark. He deposited Bradshaw for two sixes in consecutive overs. His 25th One-day hundred was his third in the World Cup, off 86 balls. There were 10 fours and 4 sixes in his 115 off 101 deliveries. The third-wicket stand with Mahela Jayawardene yielded 183. Sri Lanka totalled 303 for five. Jayasuriya had Ramnaresh Sarwan stumped by Kumar Sangakkara. He claimed two more victims, as the West Indies went into a tailspin, and crashed for 190. Jayasuriya's three wickets cost 38 runs, rounding off a splendid allround performance.

De Villiers destroys Caribbean attack

St. George's, April 10, 2007

Abraham de Villiers

For the third time Brian Lara put the opposition in. Each time his bowlers were carted above 300 runs. Once Jacques Kallis joined Abraham de Villiers, it was a veritable leather hunt. De Villiers hit two unconvincing boundaries off Darren Powell. The pair then took 15 runs off Powell. De Villiers cut Bravo to the boundary and drove over long-on for a six, raising his half-century in 58 balls. He drove Powell twice to the cover fence. They added 170. De Villiers hoisted his maiden One-day hundred in 114 balls. He suffered cramps and needed a runner. He then attacked the bowling. Chris Gayle came in the way, and de Villiers carted the first ball over mid-wicket for a six. Herschelle Gibbs struck a boundary, and again de Villiers lofted the last delivery over long-on for six. Ramnaresh Sarwan was roughed up as de Villiers slammed two consecutive deliveries into the stands over mid-wicket before dabbing the last to the point boundary. In Bravo's next over, de Villiers hit two fours past point. He departed for 146, having faced 130 deliveries and hit 12 fours and 5 sixes. De Villiers crowned his innings with a flurry of fours and sixes. Mark Boucher pillaged fifty off 21 balls. Lara took his power play in the 45th over. It cost 77 runs. South Africa finished at 356 for four. Hard as the West Indies tried, they lost by 67 runs.

Resilient Styris' lone battle against Vaas and Murali

Muttiah Muralitharan

St. George's, April 12, 2007

Like in the previous World Cup, Scott Styris played a lone hand against Sri Lanka in a lost cause. New Zealand were reeling at 4 for two, the crafty Chaminda Vaas snaring both for ducks. Vaas dismissed another later. The wily Muttiah Muralitharan spun his web, knocking one over. At 77 for four, the Kiwis were in hot waters. After a cautious start Styris hammered Farveez Maharoof. Having chipped the ball over mid-on for two runs, he drove the next wider to the fence, and punched another behind point for consecutive fours. Four overs later, Styris again slammed Maharoof for successive boundaries, eluding mid-off. He raised his fifty off 82 balls. Magical Murali struck again, trapping Brendon McCullum leg-before and having Daniel Vettori snapped up. Styris raised his century off 152 deliveries with a pull to mid-wicket, his first boundary after 97 balls. He hit the last ball of the innings from Vaas wide of long-on to the boundary. Styris was unbeaten with 111 off 157 deliveries, having hit 8 fours. New Zealand posted 219 runs. Vaas took three for 33 and Muralitharan three for 32. Sanath Jayasuriya and Kumar Sangakkara raised a 100-run second-wicket partnership. Sri Lanka sauntered to a six-wicket win. It was a fascinating battle - two top-class bowlers confronting a fighting innings by an unsung warrior of the game.

Lankans skid as Nathan Bracken jams brakes

Nathan Bracken

St. George's, April 16, 2007

It was billed as 'a final before the final'. Sri Lanka rested their war-horses Muralitharan and Vaas. The relentless left-armer Nathan Bracken tested their batting. He exploited the morning moisture, bringing one in sharply to snare Sanath Jayasuriya. McGrath too had Kumar Sangakkara lbw for a duck. In the 7th over, Bracken swung the first delivery away, which left-handed opener Upul Tharanga swished at airily. The next drifted in, and the batsman defended. The third swerved in again and beat the bat. The following delivery cut away off the seam, found a thick edge and darted towards first slip. Matthew Hayden grasped a smart low catch. Bracken's first stint was 6-2-8-2. On return he promptly delivered a maiden wicket. Slanting one just short of a length, which Nuwan Kulasekara tried to drive, he induced an edge. Hayden did an encore. Bracken bowled the last over with Sri Lanka nine down. Farveez Maharoof slogged one to the long-off boundary, and edged another to third-man. The canny Bracken deceived him with a slower ball. Maharoof swiped it to Andrew Symonds at long-on. Sri Lanka were skittled for 226. Bracken had a brilliant analysis of 9.4-3-19-4, wonderfully controlled left-arm swing that would have made Gary Gilmour proud. Australia cantered to a three-wicket win.

Andrew haul sinks England

Bridgetown, April 17, 2007

Andrew Hall

It was a high-pressure match. The winner would advance to the semi-finals. This Kensington Oval pitch had pace and bounce, and the ball swung both ways. After 33 overs England were 112 for four. Andrew Hall came on for his second spell, having already bowled five overs for 10 runs. He brought one in to Paul Collingwood, trapping him leg-before. He got another to seam in, and knock over Andrew Flintoff's middle stump. Moving the ball away from the left-handed Paul Nixon, he induced an edge into the gloves of Mark Boucher. Sajid Mahmood nicked a swinging delivery on to the stumps. The batsmen were mesmerised with his late movement and immaculate length. Hall was on a hat-trick. Monty Panesar nibbled outside the off-stump and just about managed to miss. England were reeling at 122 for eight. In this burst of three overs he had grabbed four wickets for 6 runs. Hall came on again for the 46th over in which he conceded a single. He pitched his last delivery up to James Anderson who was plumb leg-before-wicket. It was an outstanding analysis of 10-2-18-5, his only five-wicket haul in a One-day International, and the best for South Africa in the World Cup. England were bowled out for 154. Skipper Graeme Smith led from the front, plundering 89 off 58 deliveries to take South Africa forward.

Jaya-Murali show sets up final encounter

Mahela Jayawardene

Kingston, April 24, 2007

It was the first semi-final. Mahela Jayawardene strode in with Sri Lanka on 67 for two. His first boundary came off the 48th delivery. He reached his fifty off 76 balls. In the next over he hit Jacob Oram for a six, and then a Jeetan Patel full-toss for another. His hundred came off 103 deliveries with two such exquisite strokes on either side of the wicket off Oram. In the final over Jayawardene square-cut Shane Bond to the boundary and then slammed a full-toss over mid-wicket for six. Sri Lanka logged up 289 for five. Jayawardene returned unbeaten on 115 off 109 deliveries with 10 fours and 3 sixes. He had paced his innings brilliantly without ever seeming in a hurry. New Zealand threatened only when Peter Fulton and Scott Styris put on 73. After Styris' dismissal, Muttiah Muralitharan came on again and induced Oram to hit back his doosra, which the wily bowler juggled from right hand to the left and managed to hold on. The next ball was another doosra which Brendon McCullum top-edged down the throat of short fine-leg. In his following over Muralitharan trapped Daniel Vettori leg-before for a duck. Later Murali bowled Bond through the gate to finish with four for 31 off 8 overs. The last Kiwi pair swung their bats, the final flicker before the light went out.

Tait scorcher singes Proteas

Shaun Tait

Gros Islet, April 25, 2007

Shaun Tait is wild, inaccurate and expensive but has the ability to blast out the best batsmen, often when needed urgently. Ironically, he has produced successful bursts in One-dayers and Twenty20 where the mantra is accuracy. That underscores the importance of securing wickets in the shorter formats too, even if some runs are conceded. That is Tait's utility, which Australia have exploited to the hilt as in this tough semi-final. In 5.3 overs Glenn McGrath and Nathan Bracken reduced South Africa to 12 for two. Tait hurled thunderbolts at 90 miles an hour. He bounced the first, which Abraham de Villiers smashed over mid-wicket for a boundary. The fifth delivery was pitched up, de Villiers tried to drive, only to edge into the gloves of Adam Gilchrist. McGrath got two wickets off successive deliveries. South Africa were in shambles at 27 for five in 10 overs. The wayward Tait conceded 19 runs in his next two overs. Later Herschelle Gibbs despatched him square on the off-side to the boundary, but soon nicked to Gilchrist. Tait got Andrew Hall to flash, resulting in another catch for Gilchrist. He forced Andre Nel to flail, only to be taken by Michael Clarke at backward point. South Africa packed up for 149. Tait captured four wickets for 39 runs. Australia breezed to a seven-wicket win.

Star Turns

Adam's apple

Adam Gilchrist

Bridgetown, April 28, 2007

The 2007 final was a scintillating one-man show. Matthew Hayden managed just 38 in a 172-run opening stand. Adam Gilchrist was awesome. The partnership came off 22.5 overs. Rain turned it into a 38-overs-a-side game. After clipping Chaminda Vaas for four and lofting him for a six, Gilchrist slammed consecutive deliveries from Dilhara Fernando for 2 fours and a six. His fifty came off 43 balls. Blasting Tillakaratne Dilshan for two huge sixes, he rocketed Fernando for a six and on-drove him to the boundary. He then swept the great Muralitharan into the stands. Gilchrist raced to his century off 72 balls, fastest in a World Cup final, with a sizzling shot off Lasith Malinga to the ropes. He crashed Vaas twice to the fence in an over. Malinga was hammered for two successive boundaries. Gilchrist carted Sanath Jayasuriya for a six and a four. Fernando had him caught. Gilchrist's 149 was the highest in a World Cup final, and the best by a wicketkeeper. It came off 104 balls. His 8 sixes equalled the Cup record of Ricky Ponting and Imran Nazir. He smashed 13 fours besides. Australia totalled 281 for four. Sri Lanka threatened while Jayasuriya and Kumar Sangakkara added 116. Wickets tumbled and Australia triumphed in pitch darkness, a hat-trick of World Cup titles.

Legends

Andy Roberts

Andy Roberts headed the new generation of
great West Indies fast bowlers who emerged
since the mid-seventies. Roberts was one
of the finest, quick and accurate, and extremely effective in
One-day cricket too. A quiet man, with none of the petulance
of many bowlers of speed, he used his powerful shoulders
to make the ball fly. Roberts was right on the ball from the
very start, taking two for 16 off 12 overs against Sri Lanka.
Then against Pakistan he shone with the bat in that thrilling
last-wicket partnership of 64 with Deryck Murray to snatch an
astonishing win. He was back in form with the ball, capturing
three for 39 against Australia, and then two for 18 to help beat
New Zealand in the semi-final. Roberts was a vital cog in the
West Indies' title win. Again in 1979, he picked up wickets
regularly, including a three-wicket haul against New Zealand,
as the West Indies retained the Cup. He was consistent in 1983
too, bowling superbly in the final, capturing three for 32 off
10 overs as the West Indies were shocked by India. Roberts
finished with 26 World Cup wickets, a record at that time. The
conveyor belt that fetched Andy Roberts also brought in his
wake several illustrious pacemen from the Caribbean.

Wickets 26, Ave 21.23, RO 3.24, Catches nil

Vivian Richards

Vivian Richards was monarch of all he surveyed. He left his stamp on each of the first four tournaments. In 1975 he was just emerging as a top-flight batsman, but he electrified the crowd with his brilliant fielding in the final, running out Alan Turner, Greg Chappell and skipper Ian Chappell. By 1979 Richards had established himself as one of the greatest batsmen in history, adept at both versions of the game. He played an amazing knock of 138 off 157 balls in the final against England. His blistering 139-run fifth-wicket partnership with Collis King settled the issue long before the last ball was bowled. The West Indies were stunned in the opening match in 1983. In the return encounter Richards thrashed the Indian attack, scoring 119 off 146 deliveries. The next two games saw him play brilliant unbeaten knocks of 95 and 80 against Australia and Pakistan to take the West Indies to their third consecutive final. Once there, his dismissal after a cameo led to a title win by dark horses, India. Finally, in 1987 he hit the then highest World Cup score of 181 off 125 balls with 16 fours and 7 sixes against Sri Lanka. He became the first man to score 1000 runs in the premier event. He also held the record for the highest score in all One-day Internationals, a brilliant 189 not out against England in 1984 . A giant, truly.

Runs 1013, Ave 63.31, SR 85.05, Catches 9
Wickets 10, Ave 34.50, RO 4.15

Richard Hadlee

In 1975 he was still just Dayle Hadlee's younger brother, capturing just three wickets. The 1979 World Cup witnessed the legendary Richard Hadlee control. Impossible to collar, his late movement in the air and off the wicket, both ways, was awesome. He conceded only 24 runs off 12 overs to the emerging Sri Lankans and claimed a wicket. Against India, Hadlee gave away a mere 20 runs in 10 overs, dismissing openers Sunil Gavaskar and Anshuman Gaekwad. In a vain bid to upset the West Indies, Hadlee top-scored with 42. In the semi-final he removed Geoff Boycott early and conceded only 32 runs in 12 overs. By 1983 Hadlee was superlative. The English managed a mere 26 off his 12 overs as he dismissed arch rival Ian Botham. Hadlee rocked the Pakistan top-order. His analysis read 9-2-20-3. He destroyed Sri Lanka for his World Cup best of five for 25 off 10.1 overs. Three English wickets for 32 runs in 10 overs and a fine knock of 31 helped post an exciting two-wicket win with just a ball to spare. His analysis versus Sri Lanka read 12-3-16-1. His batting did not live up to the billing, but Richard Hadlee was often a one-man attack for New Zealand.

Runs 149, Ave 16.55, SR 61.06, Catches 3
Wickets 22, Ave 19.13, RO 2.88

Imran Khan

The pin-up star is perhaps the no.1 allrounder in the showpiece event, captain of the Cup-winning team in 1992 and once the leading wicket-taker. Not yet a world beater in 1975, Imran still took five wickets at 11.80 each in his two matches. By 1979 he had arrived. He bowled economically as Pakistan reached the semis. Injury prevented him from bowling in 1983 but he revelled as a batsman. A hurricane unbeaten 56 against Sri Lanka was followed by a superb unbeaten century in their return match, Pakistan's first World Cup hundred. With Pakistan at 43 for five, Imran put on 144 for the sixth wicket with Shahid Mahboob. A brilliant century stand with Zaheer Abbas, and his fine unbeaten 79, against New Zealand enabled Pakistan to advance to the semi-finals. At home in 1987 Imran bagged 17 wickets including two hauls of 4 for 37 against the West Indies and England. In the semi-final he took 3 for 36 and scored a fine 58 but could not stop Allan Border's Australians. That was put right in 1992 as Imran led Pakistan to the title after an indifferent start. A vital 72 in the final and a 139-run third-wicket stand with Javed Miandad breathed fresh life into the innings. Fittingly, he took the last wicket. That was the pinnacle as the mighty Pathan retired in a blaze of glory.

Runs 666, Ave 35.05, SR 65.61 Catches 6
Wickets 34, Ave 19.26, RO 3.86

Javed Miandad

This dogged fighter is the only player to have appeared in each of the first six World Cups. Javed Miandad was also the highest run-getter in the event, until Sachin Tendulkar surpassed him in 2003. He did not meet with spectacular success early on, but scored two fine half-centuries in 1983. In 1987 he scored a brilliant hundred against Sri Lanka which was largely responsible for victory in a closely-fought match. Along with skipper Imran Khan, he put up a fighting stand of 112 in the semi-final. But his knock of 70 off 103 balls was in vain as Australia won by 18 runs. Miandad played a key role in Pakistan's title triumph in 1992, hitting up five fifties and 437 runs at an average of 62.42. He contributed in every vital situation, topping it all with 57 off 69 balls in the semi-final, and a resilient 58 in a 139-run third-wicket partnership with Imran in the final. It was the culmination of years of hard work. A shrewd cricketing brain, Miandad's inputs played a big part in bringing home the World Cup. By 1996 he was past his best but by then was already counted amongst the greats. He could have participated in the 1999 World Cup also, as coach, but resigned shortly before the tournament began.

Runs 1083, Ave 43.32, SR 67.89, Catches 10, Stumping 1

Madan Lal

Madan Lal was a great trier, extracting the maximum from his limited resources. He bowled the first ball in the World Cup at Lord's on June 7, 1975, to England's John Jameson, and took the wicket of the first centurion, Dennis Amiss. In the cakewalk against East Africa, Madan Lal bagged three for 15 off 9.3 overs. With India tottering at 101 for six against New Zealand, he joined Abid Ali in a stand of 55. Not in the squad in 1979, Madan Lal was a key member in 1983. An unbeaten 21 and one for 34 helped India hand the West Indies their first defeat in the World Cup. He rocked Zimbabwe, capturing three for 27 in 10.4 overs. Against Australia he captured two wickets and put on 58 with Kapil Dev for the seventh wicket. With India crashing to 78 for seven against Zimbabwe, Madan Lal helped Kapil Dev add 62 runs, and then took three for 42. In the tussle against Australia for a semi-final berth, Madan Lal captured four for 20. In the final, he removed Desmond Haynes, and then struck a mortal blow as Vivian Richards skied him to be caught by Kapil Dev. Soon he had Larry Gomes caught by Sunil Gavaskar. Madan Lal's was a major role in wresting the world title.

Runs 122, Ave 30.50, SR 60.69, Catch 1
Wickets 22, Ave 19.36, RO 3.66

Michael Holding

Not for nothing was Michael Holding known
as the Rolls Royce of fast bowlers. In 1979, he
formed the famed Caribbean speed quartet
with Andy Roberts, Joel Garner and Colin Croft. Holding's
own contribution was brilliant. He had India in trouble in the
opening match, taking four for 33. Bowling accurately to New
Zealand, he conceded just 29 runs in his 12 overs, dismissing
Lance Cairns. In the semi-final against Pakistan, Holding had
Sadiq Mohammad caught behind, allowing just 28 runs off 9
overs. After Mike Brearley and Geoff Boycott laboured over
129 runs in the final, Holding dismissed both and gave away
just 16 runs in 8 overs. The 1983 edition was not easy for the
West Indies but Holding bowled beautifully. As India stunned
them, Holding bagged two for 32 in 12 overs. He took one for
23 runs in 8 overs against Australia, and two for 33 in 12 overs
versus Zimbabwe. He then captured three Indian wickets for
40 off 9.1 overs. In the semi-final against Pakistan he finished
with one for 25 in 12 overs. In the upset by India in the final,
Holding took two for 26 in 9.4 overs. He displayed superb
control and consistency conceding less than 3 runs an over and
imparting an object lesson in the art of fast bowling in One-day
cricket.

Wickets 20, Ave 17.05, RO 2.94, Catches 5

Kapil Dev

The Haryana Hurricane was still finding
his feet in international cricket in 1979. But
hardly could anyone have visualised that
Kapil Dev would strike in as dazzling a manner as he did in
1983. He hit an amazing unbeaten 175 off 138 balls with 16
fours and 6 sixes, the then record score, pulling his team out
of a dreadful morass against Zimbabwe. His 303 runs came
at an average of 60.60. He took 12 wickets at 20.41 each at an
economy-rate of 2.91. In a match that India lost to Australia, he
bagged 5 wickets for 43 and hit up a fighting 40. And he took
7 catches in the tournament, the highest in a single World Cup
till Anil Kumble bettered it by one in 1996. Finally, he lifted the
Prudential Cup after an inspired performance in the field. If
ever a captain had led from the front, it was Kapil Dev in this
event. In 1987 he was below par with the ball but batted well,
the showpiece being a stroke-filled unbeaten 72 off a mere 58
balls against New Zealand. In 1992, Kapil Dev, the bowler, was
in fairly good form in a lack-lustre Indian performance. He
will, obviously, be remembered for his deeds in 1983. He ranks
among the leading allrounder in the World Cup, with one of the
top batting strike-rates. Really, an exciting cricketer.

Runs 669, Ave 37.16, SR 115.14, Catches 12
Wickets 28, Ave 31.85, RO 3.76

Abdul Qadir

Though Sri Lankan Somachandra de Silva was a rare leg-spinner in the early days of One-day cricket, it was Abdul Qadir who showed how effective a classy practitioner of the art could be in this version too. He captured 12 wickets in each of the two World Cups that he played. Taking only 13 matches to achieve the feat, he had a strike-rate of nearly two wickets per match, remarkable for this form of cricket. He finished with an average of 21.08, had a five-wicket haul and an economy-rate of 3.72 runs per over. That set at rest all theories of leg-spinners being a dispensable commodity in Limited-overs cricket. And to imagine that India left out B. S. Chandrasekhar from their World Cup squad! In his first appearance in 1983 Qadir rocked New Zealand, taking 4 for 21 off 12 overs. But this, and his unbeaten 41, could not help Pakistan win. It was, nevertheless, an awesome allround performance. He bagged 5 for 44 against Sri Lanka, and this time his team triumphed. In 1987 he took four for 31 and three for 31 in two matches against England, and then clinched a tremendous one-wicket last ball victory over the West Indies off his bat. Imran Khan was lucky to have a man like Abdul Qadir in his team, a magical leg-spinner and a fighter to the core.

Runs 118, Ave 59.00, SR 79.72, Catches 3
Wickets 24, Ave 21.08, RO 3.72

Martin Crowe

One of the finest batsmen to have played for New Zealand, Martin Crowe made a brilliant debut in the World Cup in 1983. With his side in trouble at 62 for four, facing a huge England total of 332, he waged a lone battle to score a dominant 97. In 1987 he scored a superb 72 against Zimbabwe, and brought off the catch of the tournament to dismiss David Houghton who was causing mayhem in an attacking innings of 142. In a rain-shortened match against Australia he hit a brilliant 58 as his team went down narrowly. Another fine half-century off the Zimbabwe attack rounded off the tournament. It was in 1992 that Martin Crowe was outstanding. While his inspired captaincy helped carry the team into the semi-finals, his own form with the bat was tremendous. New Zealand won their first seven matches and Crowe hit up a century and four fifties to emerge as the man-of-the-tournament. Crowe began with a tremendous unbeaten 100 against Australia, playing more unbeaten rapid-fire innings of 74 off 44 balls, 81 off 81 and 73 not out off 81, before being run out for 91 off 83 balls in the semi-final. He finished with 456 runs at 114.00. Stephen Fleming has surpasses him as the highest rungetter for New Zealand in the World Cup, but Crowe's average and strike-rate are brilliant.

Runs 880, Ave 55.00, SR 83.49, Catches 8

Arjuna Ranatunga

The portly Sri Lankan has been one of their most durable cricketers. From an excitable youngster, Arjuna Ranatunga mellowed into a seasoned skipper who led them to a dream World Cup title win in 1996. He first appeared in 1983, but his batting sparkled in 1987. He had a run of 24, 52 not out, 40, 86 not out and 50. The fine showing continued in 1992 with a brilliant unbeaten 88 off 61 deliveries in the high-scoring win over Zimbabwe. He then engineered victory off the penultimate delivery over South Africa, hitting a tremendous unbeaten 64 off 73 balls. 1996 was special. Sri Lanka were invincible under his leadership. Ranatunga scored 241 runs for an average of 120.50, being unbeaten in four of his six innings. As Sri Lanka piled up the record score of 398 against Kenya, Ranatunga hit 75 off 40 balls, registering the then fastest fifty in the World Cup off a mere 29 balls. Brendon McCullum brought down the mark to 20 balls in 2007. In the final, Ranatunga joined Aravinda de Silva on the home stretch, hitting 47 not out off 37 deliveries. As he received the ornamental Wills World Cup, it marked the pinnacle of a glittering career. 1999 was an anti-climax. The team struggled. Ranatunga had moderate success, scoring just one fifty. But he had already done his country proud.

Runs 969, Ave 46.14, SR 80.95, Catches 7

David Boon

David Boon was a cool customer. He fought his way through the mill to become one of Australia's most dependable batsmen in the World Cup. He was a vital part of Allan Border's title-winning 1987 team. Forging a terrific opening partnership with Geoff Marsh, he hit up five fifties, plus a 49, in the tournament. His 87 off 96 balls in a 30-over game against New Zealand set up a three-run win. A 62 against India and a superb 93 against Zimbabwe reflected the brilliant form that Boon was in. In the semi-final against Pakistan at Lahore he hit a brilliant 65. Boon played the anchor's role in the final against England. He scored 75, guiding Australia to a match-winning total, and bagging the man-of-the-match award. Australia's hour of glory was also a personal triumph for David Boon. While his teammates floundered in 1992, Boon continued to display fine form. He hit up 100 in the opening match against New Zealand, and finished the tournament in exactly the same manner - with 100 off the West Indies attack. Once again he ended up with a 50-plus average. Boon's 815 runs at 54.33 were the highest for Australia in the World Cup until the Waugh twins, Ricky Ponting and Adam Gilchrist logged more. Doubtlessly, he was up there with the best.

Runs 815, Ave 54.33, SR 73.75, Catches 2

Craig McDermott

Bowlers are generally a casualty in One-day cricket. But in Australia's 1987 title triumph, Craig McDermott played a stellar role. This was not so much as a restrictive bowler, but more as one who regularly got breakthroughs to keep the pressure on the opposition. In the opening match the paceman forced defending champions India on the back foot. As the hosts were sailing at 207 for two, he struck twice to dismiss Navjot Sidhu and Dilip Vengsarkar. Later he sent back Mohammad Azharuddin and Ravi Shastri, and his haul of four for 56 proved crucial in the nail-biting one-run win. McDermott took five for 44 in the semi-final to help pip Pakistan. In the final he played his part as pinch-hitter, and was given the important task of bowling the last over in order to stop England from overhauling the Aussie total. He did it successfully, and Australia lifted the Cup for the first time. He took 18 wickets at 18.94 each, a fine performance by any yardstick. 1992 was an anti-climax but McDermott was at his restrictive best. He returned to the sub-continent in 1996 but had time to take just one wicket off three overs before injury forced him out. His 27 wickets in the World Cup place him fourth along with Steve Waugh in the list of Aussie bowlers, after Glenn McGrath, Brad Hogg and Shane Warne.

Wickets 27, Ave 22.18, RO 4.02, Catches 4

Steve Waugh

The Clint Eastwood of cricket, maybe Mr.
Determination is Steve Waugh's other name.
His reputation as 'Ice-man' took root in 1987.
Bowling the heart-stopping final over with the last Indian pair
requiring just six in the opening match, he snatched an incredible
one-run win. He repeated the feat against New Zealand, pulling
off a thrilling three-run victory. Waugh scored useful runs in
the middle and picked up wickets regularly, helping his team lift
the Cup. In 1992, it was hard times for Australia. Waugh scored
his maiden World Cup half-century, 55 off 43 balls, and got his
best haul of three for 36. In 1996 he put on 207 for the third
wicket with twin Mark against Kenya, the then biggest stand in
the World Cup. He scored 82 off 92 deliveries. He struck 57
against the West Indies. His unbeaten 59 in the quarter-final
was as vital as his stunning blow in the semi-final when he clean
bowled Brian Lara. He could not pull off such magic in the
final. That he did as captain in 1999. After a superb 62 in 61
balls off Zimbabwe, Waugh hit a brilliant unbeaten 120 off 110
balls against South Africa to carry his team into the semi-final.
He scored 56 in that exciting tied match, and then led the team
to a memorable title win. Defeat is not part of Steve Waugh's
vocabulary. Among the leading World Cup allrounders, he is
one of its brightest gems.

Runs 978, Ave 48.90, SR 81.02, Catches 14
Wickets 27, Ave 30.14, RO 4.70

Wasim Akram

One of the finest left-arm fast bowlers in history, Wasim Akram was an awesome hitter. In 1987 he was still developing. He had a whirlwind 39 and a three for 45 to his credit. In 1992, Pakistan's destiny was often linked to his performances. He had Zimbabwe reeling at 14 for two, finishing with three for 21. It was crucial to trounce the hitherto unbeaten New Zealand. Akram dismissed Andrew Jones and Martin Crowe early, bagging four for 32. In the final he blasted 33 off 19 deliveries, and dismissed Ian Botham for a duck. He swung the match, clean bowling Allan Lamb and Chris Lewis off successive balls. The crystal globe was Pakistan's. Akram played two rapid-fire knocks in 1996, but that was all. Leading in 1999, he smashed 43 off 29 balls against the West Indies. After a fine allround display against Scotland, he rocked Australia with four for 40. Pakistan made the final where they fared miserably. In 2003, he stunned the Aussies with three early strikes. But his quick-fire 33 was futile. He had rich hauls against minnows Namibia and Holland but Pakistan bowed out early. Wasim Akram was one of the craftiest pacemen ever, once the World Cup's leading wicket-taker with 55 victims, and has an awesome batting strike-rate of 100.70.

Runs 426, Ave 19.36, SR 100.70, Catches 8
Wickets 55, Ave 23.83, RO 4.04

Courtney Walsh

From back-room boy to spearhead, to ageing legend, Courtney Walsh came a long way. Keeping alive the tradition of great West Indies fast bowlers in the company of Curtly Ambrose, Walsh surpassed Andy Roberts as their leading World Cup wicket-taker with 27 victims. It was not a happy outing in 1987 as he conceded vital runs at the end of innings more than once. Ironically, his initial good work was negated as the last Pakistani pair took 14 runs off the final over. He still finished with four for 40. There was revenge in the return match as Walsh grabbed two for 34. He was absent in 1992. By 1996 he was extremely accurate and crafty. He had Kenya in trouble, taking three early wickets before disaster struck in the form of a shock defeat. He took two vital Australian wickets as the West Indies reasserted their pride. Walsh posed problems for Pakistan in 1999, taking three for 28 in 10 overs. The inexperienced Bangladesh batsmen could not handle him as he grabbed four for 25, nor could the Scots against whom he took three for 7 in 7 overs. Like vintage wine, Walsh only got better with age. Amazingly fit in the latter part of his career, his sporting conduct was as admirable as his bowling feats.

Wickets 27, Ave 20.25, RO 3.46, Catches 3

Legends

Aravinda de Silva

In the early days Aravinda de Silva would throw away his wicket with ill-judged shots, but matured into one of the best. He hit a fine 42 on debut versus Pakistan in 1987, and played a captain's knock of 62 against Australia in 1992. In 1996 his brilliance carried Sri Lanka to a title win. He trounced Zimbabwe for a superb 91 off 86 deliveries. In the record World Cup total against Kenya, de Silva hit up the highest for his country in a One-dayer - 145 off 115 balls. In the semi-final he walked in with Sri Lanka at 1 for two wickets, and played a stupendous innings. He hit 66 of the 85 runs scored while he was in, facing just 47 balls. In the final, he took three wickets for 42. Then with Sri Lanka two down for 23, de Silva hit up 50 off 50 balls, reached his hundred off 119 deliveries and stayed till the Cup was Sri Lanka's. He returned jubilant with an unbeaten 107, wrestling the man-of-the-match prize. The hero faltered in 1999. One fifty in five matches was all. In 2003, de Silva scored 41 as Kenya surprised. Hitting 73 in 78 balls off South Africa, he added 152 with Marvan Atapattu. He then took two wickets as the match was tied. A brilliant 92 off 94 balls could not stop the Aussies as he hit 9 fours and 4 sixes. De Silva became the fourth to notch 1000 runs in the World Cup.

Runs 1064, Ave 36.68, SR 86.57, Catches 14
Wickets 16, Ave 41.93, RO 4.97

Moin Khan

One of the grittiest fighters in the game, both behind and in front of the stumps, Moin Khan was a man Pakistan could always count on. Safe and vocal with the gloves on, he was resilient as well as cavalier with the bat in hand. Until Adam Gilchrist surpassed him in 2003, Moin had by far the highest dismissals in the World Cup, 30 in all, and also the maximum of 23 catches and 7 stumpings. A great motivator, Moin played several rousing knocks. He was a newcomer during Pakistan's title win in 1992. In the semi-final against New Zealand he hit a vital unbeaten 20 to usher victory in the company of the indomitable Javed Miandad. He missed the 1996 tournament but was invariably the blaster in 1999 with a scoring-rate of 110.50 runs per 100 balls, or 6.63 runs per over. He smashed the Scots for 47 off 41 balls, and trounced the Aussie attack for an unbeaten 31 in 12 deliveries with 2 fours and 3 sixes. He hit his maiden fifty against South Africa, a blistering 63 off 56 balls with 6 fours and 2 sixes. Against India he hit 34 off 37 balls. That Pakistan reached the final was in great measure due to Moin Khan. Behind the stumps, in need of quick runs, or in strife, he delivered consistently. Moin's determination to succeed was unsurpassed.

Runs 286, Ave 28.60, SR 106.31, Catches 23, Stumpings 7

Chris Harris

The One-day game is tailor-made for bit-and-pieces cricketers. On his day Chris Harris could play a dashing innings or bowl a teasingly accurate spell, but his brilliance was reflected in his fielding. In 1992 he harried Sri Lanka, snapping up three wickets for 43, and rocked Zimbabwe with three for 15. He conceded just 32 runs in 10 overs to the West Indies, removing Desmond Haynes and Gus Logie. Harris continued his fine showing against India, dismissing Sachin Tendulkar, Sanjay Manjrekar and Kapil Dev. He shared the new ball with off-spinner Dipak Patel against England and returned with two for 39. In 1996, Harris had just a three for 24 haul against Holland to show for his efforts. Then suddenly, he rose like phoenix in the quarter-final against Australia. As New Zealand slid to 44 for three, Harris and skipper Lee Germon hammered 168 runs in just 27 overs. Harris went on to hit a memorable 130 off just 124 balls with 13 fours and 4 sixes. In 1999, he scored 30 against the West Indies, and 42 against Pakistan, putting on a World Cup record seventh-wicket stand of 83 with Stephen Fleming. His bowling came to the fore with four wickets for 7 runs against first-timers Scotland. In 2003, he scored an unbeaten 38 against Canada in a match-winning stand with Scott Styris. Chris Harris is New Zealand's highest wicket-taker in the World Cup.

Runs 431, Ave 28.73, SR 68.84, Catches 7
Wickets 32, Ave 26.90, RO 4.43

Allan Donald

The great South African express was the archetypal fast bowler. Quick, aggressive, hardworking, and a fierce competitor, Allan Donald was one of the best of all time. South Africa's re-entry into international cricket came just before the 1992 World Cup. Off to a flying start against Australia, Donald captured three wickets for 34. He was at his aggressive best as he sent Sri Lanka reeling at 35 for three. He dismissed opener Krishnamachari Srikkanth for a duck and a rampaging Kapil Dev as India capitulated. In the semi-final against England, Donald sent back skipper Graham Gooch and Allan Lamb. Though plagued by injury in 1996, Donald was deadly whenever he played. First up was a veritable walkover against the United Arab Emirates. Donald took three for 21 off his 10 overs. He stopped the Kiwis in their tracks taking three for 34. Against Holland, Donald took two for 21. In 1999, Donald destroyed the England middle-order, capturing four for 17 in 8 overs. His three for 41 was in vain as Zimbabwe surprised South Africa. In the dramatic semi-final Donald and Shaun Pollock rocked Australia. Donald claimed four for 32. His run out led to the historic tie. Despite a disastrous swansong in 2003, Donald is sixth in the list of World Cup wicket-takers.

Wickets 38, Ave 24.02, RO 4.17, Catches 3

Mark Waugh

One could have gone miles to see Mark Waugh bat, inarguably the most elegant batsman of modern times. He played so late and with such exquisite timing that he made batting look so very easy. He was finding his way in 1992. With twin Steve he put on 113 off just 69 deliveries for the fifth wicket against Zimbabwe, scoring 66 not out off 39 balls. In 1996 he hit up three centuries, the first to do so in a single World Cup. He added with Steve, 207 for the third wicket against Kenya, then the highest in the World Cup. His 130 came at a-run-a-ball with 14 fours and a six. Against India he hit 3 sixes and 8 fours in his 126 off 135 balls, the only back-to-back World Cup hundreds until Rahul Dravid and Saeed Anwar emulated the feat in 1999, and Ricky Ponting and Matthew Hayden in 2007. Waugh hit an unbeaten 76 against Zimbabwe, and 30 to go with his three West Indies wickets. He made 110 in a big run-chase set up by New Zealand. In 1999, Mark Waugh became the first player to score four centuries in the World Cup with 104 against Zimbabwe. He posted 1000 runs, the fourth after Vivian Richards, Javed Miandad and Sachin Tendulkar. His 83 against India was crucial. Other useful knocks included 67 against Scotland. He guided Australia to the title with his unbeaten 37 in the final. If Steve Waugh was a fighter, Mark was a charmer.

Runs 1004, Ave 52.84, SR 83.04, Catches 11

Brian Lara

The effervescent Lara won matches off his own bat. He impressed with his strokeplay in 1992, hitting four fifties. He struck a brilliant 88 off 101 deliveries against Pakistan before retiring hurt. Smashing Zimbabwe for 72 off 71 balls, he made 52 against New Zealand. A match-winning 41 in 37 balls off India was followed by a splendid 70 against Australia. He slammed Zimbabwe again in 1996 with a 31-ball 43 not out. With the West Indies on a roller coaster ride, Lara scored 60 against Australia. He displayed real genius against South Africa, who were on a high. Crashing a tremendous 111 off only 94 balls with 16 boundaries, he carried the team into the semi-final. There he made 45 at a-run-a-ball in the narrow defeat. Skipper in 1999, Lara was not at his best with a highest score of 36 in five matches. In 2003, his superb 116 off 134 balls with 12 fours and 2 sixes demolished the Proteas. A sedate 46 against Bangladesh was followed by the then fastest fifty in the World Cup in 23 balls off Canada. He hit 73 off 40 balls with 8 fours and 5 sixes. The 2007 event at home was disappointing. A valiant 77 against the unbeatable Aussies was all, apart from some cameos. Lara is World Cup's third-highest rungetter.

Runs 1225, Ave 42.24, SR 86.26, Catches 16

Curtly Ambrose

An all-time great fast bowler, the most remarkable facet of Curtly Ambrose was pinpoint accuracy. Genuine speedsters do not find this easy as the legendary Jeff Thomson has often stated. As a result, the towering West Indian was hard to score off. In 1992 he was invariably thrifty as he took wickets regularly. But it was an unhappy tournament for the West Indies. Four years later it was sea-saw. The start was on a high as Ambrose kept Zimbabwe on a leash, taking three for 28. He pushed India on the back foot with two early wickets before the hosts sped away. In the humiliating defeat by Kenya, Ambrose bowled as well as ever, picking up two for 21 off 8.3 overs, and against Australia he conceded just 25 runs in 10 overs. Again in the quarter-final he was difficult to get away and took a customary early wicket. In the semi-final, he and Ian Bishop shattered the Australian top order, reducing them to 15 for four. He finished with two for 26. In 1999 it was vintage Ambrose, impossible to collar. Though the West Indies floundered, he sent Australia reeling again. He took three for 31. He and Courtney Walsh kept the flag fluttering even in difficult times. The 6 feet 7 inches tall Curtly Ambrose was a true giant on the field.

Wickets 24, Ave 20.79, RO 3.03, Catch 1

Sachin Tendulkar

Boy wonder Sachin Tendulkar's 54 not out in the win over Pakistan, 81 in 77 balls against Zimbabwe, and 84 off New Zealand were a fine initiation in 1992. In 1996, he hit 127 not out off Kenya, posting 163 with Ajay Jadeja, India's best World Cup opening stand. Tendulkar revelled in an unbeaten 70 off the West Indies, and 90 in 84 balls against Australia. He blasted a-run-a-ball 137 off Sri Lanka, adding 175 with Mohammad Azharuddin, and compiled 65 in the semi-final with the same team. Sadly in 1999, his father passed away. He came back, slamming 140 not out in 101 balls off Kenya, adding an unbroken 237 with Rahul Dravid. Inspirational in 2003, he hit 469 runs in the six pool matches. It comprised 81 against Zimbabwe, his high of 152 and second-best World Cup stand of 244 with Sourav Ganguly off Namibia, an explosive 98 in 75 balls annihilating Pakistan, and fifties against Holland and England. He signed off with 97 against Sri Lanka, and a semi-final 83 off Kenya, wresting the Golden Bat player-of-the-tournament prize. The 2007 World Cup was a disaster. A rapid-fire unbeaten 57 against lowly Bermuda was all. India capsized early. His 673 runs in 2003, aggregate of 1796, and eight man-of-the-match awards stand out. Tendulkar is on a pedestal all his own.

Runs 1796, Ave 57.93, SR 88.21, Catches 10

Javagal Srinath

Successor to Kapil Dev, Javagal Srinath was learning the ropes in 1992, two for 23 being his best. In 1996 he was the spearhead. He dealt the West Indies two stunning blows, dismissing Sherwin Campbell and Brian Lara cheaply. Against Zimbabwe he picked up two for 36. A lone star in a disastrous semi-final, he reduced in-form Sri Lanka to two down for 1, dismissing Romesh Kaluwitharana and Sanath Jayasuriya. He removed Asanka Gurusinha too. But the Lankans broke away. Srinath took three for 34. He rocked South Africa in 1999, dismissing Gary Kirsten and Herschelle Gibbs early. He picked up two Zimbabwean wickets and seemed to be pulling off an exciting victory with the bat. He had smashed 18 off 12 balls with 2 sixes but fell to a rash shot. He continued to bowl tidily and struck vital blows against Pakistan, ending with three for 37. Extremely dangerous at the start of innings, Javagal Srinath's Achilles' heel was his inability to check the run-rate. By 2003, he exercised great control. After a World Cup best of four for 30 against Holland, he dismissed the Zimbabwean openers cheaply. In his finest stint, he took four quick wickets as Sri Lanka crashed to 40 for five. Srinath is the fifth-highest wicket-taker in the World Cup.

Wickets 44, Ave 27.81, RO 4.32, Catches 4

Sanath Jayasuriya

Sanath Jayasuriya scored 32 in the record win over Zimbabwe in 1992. In 1996, he and Romesh Kaluwitharana raised 53 in five overs off India. Jayasuriya hit 79 off 76 balls. Against Kenya, the pair sped to 50 off 20 balls, raising 83 off 40 deliveries. Jayasuriya's 44 off 27 balls had 3 sixes and 5 fours. In the quarter-final, he slammed England for 82 off 44 balls with 13 fours and 3 sixes, then joint fastest World Cup fifty off 30 balls. He took three for 12 as India collapsed in the semi-final. He won an Audi car as player-of-the-tournament in the title triumph. In 1999 Jayasuriya's best was 39 off Kenya. Captain in 2003, he posted 170 with Hashan Tillekeratne against the Kiwis, hammering 120 off 125 balls with 14 fours. He was 55 not out as Bangladesh floundered. He contributed to wins, scoring 66 against West Indies, and taking three Zimbabwe wickets for 30. In 2007 he scored 109 against Bangladesh with 7 fours and 7 sixes, racing to his hundred in 85 balls. His 115 off 101 deliveries and three wickets for 38 toppled West Indies. A vital 64 helped beat the Kiwis. His 63 in the final was futile. He is fourth-highest with 1165 runs at a strike-rate of 90.66, has 27 wickets and five man-of-the-match awards.

Runs 1165, Ave 34.26, SR 90.66, Catches 18
Wickets 27, Ave 39.25, RO 4.83

Legends

Muttiah Muralitharan

Muttiah Muralitharan was initially a massive turner of the ball. His action often questioned, he developed subtle variations to become a world-beater. In the World Cup triumph of 1996 he conceded under four runs an over. His best was two for 37 in the quarter-final win over England. He was a vital performer. By 1999, Murali was near his best. He bagged three for 25 against South Africa, scalping Daryll Cullinan, Jonty Rhodes and Shaun Pollock. The Lankans had an unhappy run as holders in 1999. Four years later, Murali was the highest wicket-taker among spinners with 17 scalps in a World Cup dominated by fast bowlers. He took three for 25 against Bangladesh, and four for 28 in the upset by Kenya. His three for 46 could not stop India. Sri Lanka reached the semi-finals. In 2007 he bagged three for 41 against India and three for 34 against the Proteas. In the annihilation of the Kiwis and the Irish, Murali bagged three and four wickets respectively. He created mayhem in the semi-final with four New Zealand wickets for 31 runs. The final was Adam Gilchrist's show. Murali was second-highest with 23 wickets. He is third-highest wicket-taker in the World Cup with 53 wickets, and a brilliant average of 19.69 and economy-rate of 3.83. Murali redefined the frontiers of off-spin bowling.

Wickets 53, Ave 19.69, RO 3.83, Catches 12

Chaminda Vaas

A combative cricketer and a great trier, Chaminda Vaas produced sporadic bursts of brilliance. In the triumphant 1996 campaign, he played his part quietly while the seniors cornered the glory. He was invariably on target, took the odd wicket or two, and played a useful knock when he got a chance. Sri Lanka were lacklustre in 1999. Again Vaas gave vital breakthroughs and struck quick cameos. In 2003 he operated on a different plane. Having bagged a record One-day haul of eight for 19 the previous season, he now captured 23 wickets, the highest ever in a World Cup then. He took a hat-trick off the first three balls of the match against Bangladesh, then a fourth wicket off the fifth ball. He scalped six for 25, Sri Lanka's best analysis in the World Cup. There were stints of three for 15, three for 41, and four for 22 in succession against Canada, Kenya and West Indies respectively. He bagged seven wickets in the last three matches. The team lost to Australia in the semi-finals. In 2007 he invariably prised out a wicket or two early in the innings, and bowled significant spells as Sri Lanka finished runners-up. He grabbed three Kiwi wickets for 33. Vaas is the fourth-highest wicket-taker in the World Cup. His batting was often handy and belligerent.

Runs 219, Ave 21.90, SR 73.98, Catches 7
Wickets 49, Ave 21.22, RO 3.97

Shane Warne

Leg-spinning great Shane Warne spurred Australia to successive World Cup finals, and had a big hand in the title win in 1999.

Among spinners, he was the leading wicket-taker in the event with 32 scalps at under 4 runs an over, until Muttiah Muralitharan and Brad Hogg passed him. After thrifty bowling in the first two matches in 1996 he rocked Zimbabwe, taking four for 34 off 9.3 overs. In the high-scoring quarter-final, Warne took two New Zealand wickets, then blasted 24 off 14 balls as pinch-hitter. In the semi-final, the West Indies were coasting at 165 for two, needing 208. Warne struck, claiming three quick wickets. West Indies collapsed for 202. Warne bagged four for 36. Scotland succumbed to his wiles in 1999. He took three for 39. He flummoxed the West Indies, bagging three for 11 off 10 overs. Warne scalped two for 33 against South Africa. He struck repeatedly in the stunning semi-final tie. The team was buoyed as he captured four for 29. The final was a cakewalk. Warne spun his magic around Pakistan with four for 33. He was man-of-the-match in the semi-final and final, like Mohinder Amarnath and Aravinda de Silva earlier. A positive drug test put him out of the 2003 event. Such aberrations apart, Shane Warne was special. His big leg-spinners and deadly flippers left batsmen mesmerised.

Wickets 32, Ave 19.50, RO 3.83, Catches 2

Ricky Ponting

Ricky Ponting became the youngest World Cup centurion in 1996. This 102 off the West Indies came in 111 balls. Helping skipper Mark Taylor add 101 off 115 balls in the final, Ponting hit 45. Sri Lanka triumphed. He played two knocks of 47 in successive defeats in 1999. Ponting assisted Steve Waugh add a crucial 126 against South Africa, scoring 69. Australia lifted the World Cup. Skipper in 2003, Ponting took 53 off Pakistan. He hit 114 off 109 balls against Sri Lanka, including century stands with Adam Gilchrist and Damien Martyn. His 140 not out, unbroken 234-run third-wicket stand with Martyn and total of 359 were records in a World Cup final. He bludgeoned India for 8 sixes, a Cup maximum, and 4 fours in 121 balls. Australia retained the title. In 2007 against Scotland he scored his fourth World Cup hundred. He hit a-run-a-ball 91 in the run-feast off South Africa, and was run out for 86 against England. An unbeaten 66 ushered victory over Sri Lanka, followed by another 66 off the Kiwis. Australia completed a hat-trick of titles, and a string of 22 victories in two World Cups under Ponting. It was his best World Cup with 539 runs. Having the second-highest aggregate of 1537 runs, after Tendulkar, his 39 matches and 25 catches are records.

Runs 1537, Ave 48.03, SR 81.06, Catches 25

Glenn McGrath

The lanky Glenn McGrath's line was one of the straightest. In 1996, he was economical, taking two vital wickets in the quarter-final with the Kiwis. With the West Indies cruising in the semi-final, McGrath effected two vital breakthroughs. The slide began. In 1999, McGrath decimated the West Indies, grabbing five for 14 off 8.4 overs. He stunned India, dismissing Tendulkar for a duck, Dravid for 2 and Azharuddin for 3. In the final he took two for 13 in 9 overs. In 2003, McGrath destroyed Namibia, capturing seven for 15, best-ever World Cup figures. He blew away the Kiwi top, securing three wickets. Another three-wicket haul against India took his tally to 21 in this event. McGrath took wickets regularly in the group matches of 2007. Four consecutive three-wicket hauls in the super-eights were debilitating for the West Indies, Bangladesh, England and Ireland. A couple of wickets each against Sri Lanka and New Zealand were followed by another bag of three South African wickets in the semi-final. With a scalp in the final he took his tally to a record 26 in the tournament, with wickets in every match. The top wicket-taker in the premier event with 71 victims, McGrath holds the record of 39 appearances with Ponting. He formed one of the most lethal combinations in history with Shane Warne.

Wickets 71, Ave 18.19, RO 3.96, Catches 5

Anil Kumble

Anil Kumble's heavily top-spun deliveries make him an unusual operator. Devastating on the slow turners at home, he remained an enigma overseas. He was a star in 1996, snaring not only the maximum 15 wickets but also clutching the most catches, 8 in all. The Kenyans found Kumble difficult to handle as he captured three for 28. The West Indies too were bemused as he scythed through the middle, taking three for 35. Even as the Sri Lankans went on a rampage, Kumble dismissed the in-form Sanath Jayasuriya and Aravinda de Silva. He picked up two more wickets against Zimbabwe, and delivered the knockout punch at Pakistan in the electrifying quarter-final, grabbing three wickets. In 1999 he took two wickets each in the disaster against Zimbabwe, and the inspired display versus England. He repeated the feat in the memorable win over Pakistan. Kumble played only three matches in 2003, bagging his best of four for 32 against Holland. In India's disastrous 2007 campaign, Kumble appeared only once against no-hopers Bermuda, scalping three easy victims. He is India's second-highest wicket-taker in the World Cup after Javagal Srinath. In the nineties, Indian hopes invariably rose and fell in direct relation to Kumble's bowling performances. Unplayable one day, innocuous the next, he was India's pride - and despair - but ever the fighter.

Wickets 31, Ave 22.83, RO 4.08, Catches 14

Saeed Anwar

Scintillating strokeplayer, Saeed Anwar was deemed fit only for the One-day game. But the left-hander proved to be a man for all seasons, one of the finest openers in the world. Pakistan's campaign in the 1996 World Cup began with two simple outings against the minnows, UAE and Holland, and Anwar obliged with unbeaten knocks of 40 and 83. He flayed the English attack for 71 runs and was run out for 62 against New Zealand. Facing India in a supercharged quarter-final, Anwar and skipper Aamir Sohail made a terrific bid for the huge target of 288. Anwar fell for 48 off just 32 balls after an opening stand of 84 in 10 overs, and Pakistan floundered. After some moderate scores in 1999, Anwar hit an electrifying hundred in the last super-six match. He flayed the Zimbabwe attack for a superb 103, and raised 95 for the first wicket with Wajahatullah Wasti. Anwar then emulated Mark Waugh and Rahul Dravid in scoring back-to-back centuries, as he hit an unbeaten 113 in the one-sided semi-final against New Zealand. This time he and Wasti raised 194, a World Cup record. The final was forgettable. The 2003 campaign went awry. Anwar's classy 101 was not enough to beat India. Pakistan bowed out but. He had the record score of 194 in One-dayers until Sachin Tendulkar hit the first double century.

Runs 915, Ave 53.82, SR 79.08, Catches 3

Jacques Kallis

Jacques Kallis was anonymous during the 1996 Cup. In 1999 he scored 96 against India and grabbed three early Sri Lankan wickets to set up victories. Two quick scalps stunned England. After an unbeaten 44 against Kenya, Kallis scored a resilient 54 off Pakistan before dismissing both openers cheaply to register more successes. In the pulsating semi-final Kallis claimed Adam Gilchrist and complied 53. The teams finished level in that last-over drama. The Proteas bowed out but Kallis was brilliant. The 2003 event at home was disastrous. His highest was 33. In the disastrous tie with Sri Lanka, Kallis took three for 41, his only wickets. The Proteas crashed out early. In 2007, century stands with Graeme Smith, Herschelle Gibbs - who smashed 6 sixes in an over - and Mark Boucher marked Kallis' 128 off Netherlands. He scored a vain 48 against Australia. In the cliff-hanger with Sri Lanka, Kallis' crucial 86 helped clinch a one-wicket win despite Lasith Malinga's four wickets in a row. After 66 off the Irish, Kallis fell for 32 in the upset by Bangladesh. An 86-ball 81, 170-run stand with Abraham de Villiers, and two wickets including Brian Lara helped trounce the West Indies. There was little joy thereafter. South Africa lost the semi-final. Kallis had a wonderful stint. He has been workmanlike for South Africa.

Runs 923, Ave 51.27, SR 74.79, Catches 7
Wickets 16, Average 48.81, RO 4.31

Steve Tikolo

Facing India in 1996, Tikolo scored 65, adding 96 with Maurice Odumbe. He top-scored again with 29 in the stunning upset of the West Indies. After Sri Lanka piled up a record 398 for five, Tikolo put on 137 with Hitesh Modi, being yorked for 96 off 95 deliveries with 8 fours and 4 sixes. It was a superb effort for a first-timer. In 1999 against England Tikolo raised 100 with Ravindu Shah, scoring a fine 71. He top-scored again with 58 against India, hoisting 118 with Kennedy Otieno. He had the highest aggregate for Kenya again. Captain in 2003, he was now a regular off-spinner. He scored 42 runs off 49 deliveries against Canada. Tikolo grabbed two wickets, conceding just 13 runs in the brilliant win over Sri Lanka. A 27 and three for 14 helped clinch the Bangladesh game. Tikolo wrested two cheap Zimbabwe wickets, and scored 51 against the powerful Australians. In Kenya's first semi-final he dismissed Tendulkar and then carved 56 runs. In 2007 Tikolo bagged two wickets for 34 and returned unbeaten with 72 off 76 balls to engineer a win over Canada. He complied a valiant 76 against England. Kenya were out of the tournament but Tikolo topped the batting as well as bowling averages for his team. Steve Tikolo is the hero of Kenyan cricket.

Runs 724, Ave 34.47, SR 69.48, Catches 10
Wickets 14, Average 28.21, RO 5.30

Adam Gilchrist

Adam Gilchrist blitzed Bangladesh in 1999 for 63 off 39 balls, raising 98 with Mark Waugh. They hoisted 97 against India, Gilchrist pouching four catches too. He hit Pakistan for the fastest fifty in a World Cup final off 33 balls, the opening stand realising 75 in 10.1 overs. In 2003 he notched 100 upfront with Hayden off India. They raised 89 against Zimbabwe, Gilchrist hitting 61 off 64 balls. He caught six Namibians, a World Cup best. Gilchrist realised 75 with Hayden and 106 with Ponting against Sri Lanka, being run out for 99 off 88 balls. He slammed Kenya for 67 in 43 balls. Gilchrist blasted India in the final for 57 off 48 balls, slamming 105 in 14 overs with Hayden. There were blazing opening stands with Hayden in the three group matches in 2007. It was the same in many super-eight games, Gilchrist getting half-centuries or thereabouts. After pouching four catches in the penultimate game, Gilchrist hammered Sri Lanka in the final for a hundred in 72 balls, the opening stand bludgeoning 172 runs. Gilchrist plundered 149 off 104 deliveries with 13 fours and 8 sixes, highest in a World Cup final and by a wicketkeeper. His 52 dismissals are a World Cup record, and with over a thousand runs and strike-rate above 98, make him an immortal.

Runs 1085, Ave 36.16, SR 98.01, Catches 45, Stumpings 7

Lance Klusener

A scintillating hitter, Lance Klusener was often devastating with his open chested fast-medium bowling. He was man-of-the-tournament in the 1999 World Cup for a stunning act: three for 66, and 12 not out (4 balls, 3 fours); 52 not out (45 balls, 5 fours, 2 sixes), and three for 21; 48 not out (40 balls, 3 fours, 1 six), and one for 16 off 6 overs; five for 21 off 8.3 overs; one for 36, and 52 not out (58 balls, 3 fours, 2 sixes); one for 41, and 46 not out (41 balls, 3 fours, 3 sixes); 4 (5 balls, 1 four), and two for 46; 36 (21 balls, 4 fours, 1 six), and one for 53; and none for 50, and 31 not out (16 balls, 4 fours, 1 six) in the historic semi-final tie. Klusener powered to 281 runs in 8 knocks (average 140.50) at a strike-rate of 122.17 runs (7.33 runs per over), slamming 26 fours and 10 sixes. He captured 17 wickets at 20.59 each, conceding 4.61 runs per over. South Africa floundered in 2003. Klusener blasted 57 (48 balls, 5 fours, 1 six) against the West Indies, and 33 not out (21 balls, 4 fours, 1 six) off New Zealand. He bagged four Kenyan wickets for 16. Signing off with the best World Cup run-rate of 121.17, Klusener was simply irresistible. He has an amazing allround quotient - batting average divided by bowling average - of 5.60 in the event.

Runs 372, Ave 124.00, SR 121.17, Catches 2
Wickets 22, Ave 22.13, RO 4.82

Mark Boucher

Mark Boucher snapped up Sachin Tendulkar in 1999 and scored 34 off 36 deliveries. He effected three dismissals, including a run out against Pakistan before ushering in victory with the bat. He pouched four catches in the tied semi-final. In 2003 Boucher pocketed a couple of catches and struck a-run-a-ball 49 in the three-run loss to the West Indies. After slamming Muralitharan for a six, Boucher was asked to play the last ball safely, with rain imminent. But South Africa were horrified that they had tied with Sri Lanka, and bowed out. Boucher was unbeaten with 45. He held another 11 catches. As Gibbs lashed out 6 sixes in an over off Dutch Daan van Bunge in 2007, Boucher crashed the then fastest World Cup fifty in 21 balls. He scored 75 not out off just 31 deliveries, blasting 9 boundaries and 4 sixes, and adding an unbroken 134 in 9.1 overs with Jacques Kallis. As Australia logged 377 for six, Boucher did not concede a single bye, the second-highest World Cup total without a bye. With Brendon McCullum taking away his World Cup record of fastest fifty by one ball, Boucher bludgeoned a half-century in 21 balls again, off the West Indies. Australia knocked out the Proteas in the semi-final. Reliable behind the stumps, Boucher's belligerent batting has been a bonus.

Runs 381, Ave 27.21, SR 94.07, Catches 31, Stumping nil

Herschelle Gibbs

Exhilarating batsman and fielder, Herschelle
Gibbs hoisted the 1999 event's first century
opening stand with Gary Kirsten, scoring
60 against England. They decimated New Zealand, raising
176, Gibbs carving 91 off 118 balls. He hit 101 in 134 balls
off Australia but his grassing of Steve Waugh cost dear. The
Proteas were knocked out in the tied semi-final. Gibbs was
banned in the match-fixing saga. In 2003 Gibbs and Kirsten
blitzed 142 in 21.2 overs to annihilate Kenya. Gibbs slammed
87 off 66 balls with 12 fours and 4 sixes. He hit 143 in 141 balls
with 19 fours and 3 sixes but New Zealand skipper Stephen
Fleming carried the day. Gibbs and Kirsten rattled 109 in 12
overs off Bangladesh. Gibbs hit 73 off 88 balls against Sri
Lanka, but the Proteas exited again after a tie. He bludgeoned
6 sixes in a Daan van Bunge over in 2007, his 72 off the Dutch
spanning 40 deliveries. In the upset by Bangladesh he scored a
vain unbeaten 59. In a rollicking stand of 86 in 6.1 overs with
Mark Boucher against the West Indies, Gibbs crashed 61 not
out off 40 balls. He scored 60 in the defeat to the Kiwis, and
went down fighting in the semi-final battle with Australia. He is
South Africa's top run-getter in the World Cup.

Runs 1067, Ave 56.15, SR 87.38, Catches 10

Geoff Allott

Left-armer Geoff Allott had a dream World Cup in 1999. With a springy run-up and pronounced follow-through reminiscent of England's medium-pacer John Lever, he moved the ball disconcertingly to come up with vital breakthroughs. Allott had debutants Bangladesh reeling at 7 for two before completing the final rites. He finished with three for 30 off 8.4 overs. Allott was the destroyer in the stunning upset of Australia. He trapped Mark Waugh leg-before, had Adam Gilchrist caught, and bowled the dangerous Michael Bevan and Shane Warne. Allott took four for 37 off 10 overs. Even as Pakistan marched on, he bagged four of their wickets for 64. The Scots found him too wobbly as he grabbed three for 15 off 10 overs. Fifteen wickets in five league matches was brilliant. Allott's strike-rate remained at par in the super-six match against Zimbabwe. He captured three for 24 in 10 overs. His 18 wickets equalled the then record for a single World Cup. The wicket of South African Herschelle Gibbs took Allott to the pinnacle. He ended the campaign with 20 wickets, a mark equalled by the peerless Shane Warne in the final. It was surpassed in 2003 and 2007. But the world sat up and took notice of Geoff Allott in 1999.

Wickets 20, Ave 16.25, RO 3.70, Catch 1

Neil Johnson

Allrounder Neil Johnson emerged as one of the brightest stars in the 1999 World Cup. Bowling his right-arm seamers, Johnson dismissed Kenyan opener Kennedy Otieno, and star batsman Steve Tikolo. He castled Hitesh Modi and Thomas Odoyo, grabbing four for 42. Left-handed Johnson opened the batting and hit up 59 off 70 balls with 7 fours and 2 sixes. Zimbabwe won by five wickets. He played a lead role as his side rocked South Africa. His knock of 76 off 117 balls comprised 10 boundaries. Then he caused a sensation, having Gary Kirsten caught off the first ball of the innings. He soon dismissed Jacques Kallis and skipper Hansie Cronje. South Africa slumped to 40 for six. Johnson finished with three for 27 off eight overs. Zimbabwe won by 48 runs. In the super-six, Australia slammed 303 runs. Johnson removed Adam Gilchrist and centurion Mark Waugh for figures of two for 43. And in a brilliant batting display, Johnson hit a spectacular unbeaten 132 off 144 deliveries with 14 fours and 2 sixes. Zimbabwe lost, but Johnson shone. Unable to bowl against Pakistan, he played a lone hand with an innings of 54. Zimbabwe were knocked out but Johnson's brilliance facilitated their best World Cup display to date. Alas, he soon opted out of the lacklustre team.

Runs 367, Ave 52.42, SR 73.99, Catch 1
Wickets 12, Ave 19.41, RO 4.66

Sourav Ganguly

Sourav Ganguly hit 97 on Cup debut, his 100th One-dayer. His 183 off Sri Lanka, India's best in One-dayers then, was second in the World Cup to Gary Kirsten's 188. He hit 17 fours off 158 balls, his 7 sixes matching Vivian Richards' World Cup and Tendulkar's Indian record at the time. He added 318 for the second wicket with Dravid, first One-day 300-run stand. Ganguly's 40 and three for 27 trounced England. Captain in 2003, he took three Zimbabwe wickets for 22. Adding 244 with Tendulkar against Namibia, Ganguly hit 112 not out off 119 balls with 6 fours and 4 sixes. His unbeaten 107 off 120 balls inspired a super-six win over Kenya. He took 48 off Sri Lanka. His unconquered 114-ball semi-final knock of 111 had 5 fours and 5 sixes. Like Mark Waugh and Matthew Hayden he carved three hundreds in a World Cup. India lost the final, Ganguly's 100th One-dayer as skipper, but achieved eight successive wins. He scored a pedestrian 66 in the upset by Bangladesh in 2007, and 89 off Bermuda, exclusively featuring in three double-century stands in the event by adding a second-wicket 202 with Sehwag. He has four centuries, most in the World Cup, with Mark Waugh, Tendulkar and Ponting. Magnificent on flat tracks, vulnerable against top pace, Ganguly had many avtaars.

Runs 1006, Ave 55.88, SR 77.50, Catch 1
Wickets 10, Average 30.50, RO 4.91

Rahul Dravid

The technician who turned dasher, took all by surprise in 1999. Dravid was the highest run-getter with 461 runs at 65.85. A cultured 54 against South Africa, and a 130-run second-wicket stand with Sourav Ganguly marked his World Cup debut. The maiden hundred, an unbeaten 104 with 10 fours, came up against Kenya, with an unbroken third-wicket 237-run partnership with Tendulkar. Dravid and Ganguly put on 318 for the second wicket against holders Sri Lanka, highest for any wicket in the World Cup and in all One-dayers. Dravid's 145 off 129 deliveries had 17 fours and a six. He also kept wickets in the match. In the crucial outing versus England, Dravid hit 53. He top-scored with 61 in the needle encounter with Pakistan. Dravid was a star in difficult batting conditions. Resilient knocks, crucial stands and wicketkeeping were Dravid's forte in 2003. An unbeaten 43 off Zimbabwe preceded a vital 62 and three catches against England. His 44 not out clinched victory over Pakistan. Dravid's dogged 32 arrested a slide in a super-six battle with Kenya. His undefeated 53 brought up a win over New Zealand. In the final his 47 was in vain. Captain of a voyage gone awry in 2007, Dravid scored a desperate 60 in the futile chase of Sri Lanka. He has been a team-man to the core.

Runs 860, Ave 61.42, SR 74.97, Catches 17, Stumping 1

Matthew Hayden

As India presented a small target in 2003, Matthew Hayden and Adam Gilchrist raised 100 in 17.3 overs. After a couple of cameos, Hayden hit 88 off Namibia. With Gilchrist he raised 105 runs off 14 overs in the final against India, but contributed just 37. The spark was missing for the most part. Australia wrested the title. Hayden's bat blazed away in 2007. After two useful opening partnerships off the minnows, the exhilarating pair hoisted 106 in 14.5 overs against South Africa. Hayden beat John Davison's mark by slamming a hundred off 66 balls, blitzing 14 fours and 4 sixes. Australia logged their highest World Cup total. Hayden hit a successive hundred, his 158 off the West Indies being the top Cup score for Australia, facing just 143 deliveries and blasting 14 fours and 4 sixes. Hayden and Gilchrist clocked a 10-wicket triumph over Bangladesh, racing to 106 in 13.5 overs. After a couple of useful performances, Hayden added 137 with Ricky Ponting against the Kiwis. He reached his third hundred of the tournament, bludgeoning 103 in 100 balls. Hayden scored 41 in the semi-final. As Gilchrist annihilated Sri Lanka in the final, Hayden notched 38 runs in an association of 172. Australia were champions again. Hayden's was the highest aggregate of 659 runs, 14 short of Tendulkar's 2003 record.

Runs 987, Ave 51.94, SR 92.93, Catches 7

Brett Lee

In the pool matches of the 2003 event, Brett
Lee had just one good stint of three for 36
against India. His 160.7 kph express against
England was the quickest save a Shoaib Akhtar 161.3 kph streak
of lightning. Lee was devastating from the super-sixes onwards.
He fractured Sanath Jayasuriya's thumb with a nasty lifter, and
tore into the Sri Lankan line-up with three quick wickets. The
Kiwis hit 31 off his first five overs. Lee struck back with five
wickets for 11, including three in four balls, in a spell of 4.1
overs. Kenya now bore the brunt. A thunderbolt hit Kennedy
Otieno's elbow and dislodged the bails. Brijal Patel edged to
Ricky Ponting. David Obuya was bowled by an in-swinging
yorker. It was the fourth hat-trick of the World Cup, following
the feats of Chetan Sharma, Saqlain Mushtaq and Chaminda
Vaas. Lasith Malinga went one better in 2007. Lee finished
with 8-3-14-3. He blasted out Sri Lanka again in the semi-
final, capturing three for 35. In the final he took two for 31.
His 22 wickets were the highest for Australia in a World Cup,
surpassing Warne's 20 in 1999, and one less than Chaminda
Vaas' record tally then. Brett Lee was a smiling assassin for his
brutal speed and unfettered jubilation at the gunning down of
batsmen.

Wickets 22, Ave 17.90, RO 4.73, Catches 8

Brad Hogg

Brad Hogg helped the belligerent Andrew Symonds add 70 in 9.3 overs against Pakistan in 2003, and then struck in the middle, grabbing three wickets for 54. He took three Zimbabwe wickets for 46. He had 2 two-wicket hauls against Sri Lanka, in the super-six and semi-final. Australia took the Cup. In the lung opener against Scotland in 2007, Hogg smashed his highest World Cup score, 40 not out off 15 balls. He clouted Dougie Brown for 24 runs in the final over. Hogg ran through the Dutch tail, grabbing four wickets for 27. After Matthew Hayden blasted the fastest World Cup hundred off the Proteas, Hogg captured three top-order wickets for 61. Versus the West Indies, he again prised out crucial wickets, including Brian Lara, finishing with three for 56. Hogg dismissed the two highest Sri Lankan scorers, Mahela Jayawardene and Chamara Silva, bagging two for 35. In the huge victory over New Zealand, Hogg captured four for 29. As Sanath Jayasuriya and Kumar Sangakkara challenged in the final, Hogg dismissed the latter. Australia completed a hat-trick of World Cup titles. His 21 wickets in 11 matches at an average of 15.80 and economy-rate of 4 runs an over are enviable. Ideal foil to the pacemen, Hogg is the second-highest wicket-taker for Australia in the World Cup after Glenn McGrath.

Wickets 34, Ave 19.23, RO 4.12, Catches 8

Kumar Sangakkara

All Kumar Sangakkara managed in the 2003 World Cup were a few cameos. Run out for 20 against the rampaging Australians, he got 30 off India and hit the Zimbabweans for a 25-ball 35. On the tricky St. George's Park pitch, Sangakkara brought off three catches and a stumping and scored an unbeaten 39. To be fair, he batted mostly at no. 6, either fighting with his back to the wall or required to accelerate the scoring. He did a commendable job behind the sticks, claiming 17 victims. In 2007 Sangakkara achieved his highest World Cup score of 76 against Bermuda. He carved 56 off 55 balls from the Bangladesh bowlers, then took three catches. Against New Zealand, Sangakkara put on a hundred with Sanath Jayasuriya in a polished unbeaten 69. Adam Gilchrist batted Sri Lanka out of the final with a breathtaking century. Sangakkara added 116 for the second wicket with Jayasuriya, striking 54 off 52 deliveries with 6 fours and a six. But Sri Lanka faded away quickly, just as the light did, and Australia lifted their third straight World title. Sangakkara is only the second player after the matchless Adam Gilchrist to score 500 runs and claim 30 victims behind the stumps in this showpiece event, though a batsman of his calibre should have a better record.

Runs 526, Ave 30.94, SR 74.71, Catches 26, Stumping 6

Scott Styris

Scott Styris struck a brilliant hundred in a losing battle on World Cup debut in 2003, after Sanath Jayasuriya's superb 120 for Sri Lanka. He blazed 141 off 125 balls, tonking 6 sixes. Styris played two unbeaten knocks to usher in victory over minnows Bangladesh and Canada. He had an average above 50 and strike-rate over 100 in the event. Styris featured in an unfinished partnership of 138 with Jacob Oram in the triumph over England in 2007. He was unbeaten with 87 in 113 deliveries. With two 80-plus stands, Styris scored 63 off 62 balls in the annihilation of Kenya. He hit a classy unbeaten 80 off 90 balls while defeating the West Indies, adding an unfinished 102 with Craig McMillan. Styris struck with the ball as Bangladesh flopped, grabbing four wickets for 43, his World Cup best. He played another valiant knock in the face-off with Sri Lanka, scoring 111 not out off 157 deliveries. Cruising to 56 in the victory over South Africa, he played a cameo in the semi-final as the Lankans prevailed. Styris had an average and strike-rate above 83, with a hundred and 4 fifties in this edition. He has a brilliant record with the highest average among the top 59 rungetters in the World Cup, and a strike-rate close to 90. Add 13 wickets and you have a priceless asset.

Runs 767, Ave 69.72, SR 89.09, Catches 10
Wickets 13, Average 32.69, RO 4.63

Shane Bond

When New Zealand met Sri Lanka in 2003, Bond bagged two wickets for 44. He took three for 33 in the cakewalk over Bangladesh. Even as John Davison fired a 25-ball fifty, Bond wrested three Canadian scalps for 29. He bowled with fire at the rampaging Australians, reducing the champions to 84 for seven at one stage. Bond had a brilliant return of six wickets for 23, the best World Cup analysis for the Kiwis. He stunned India with two early wickets. It was a fine tournament as he bagged 17 wickets at 17.94 apiece with an economy-rate of 3.91. He was bang on target in the 2007 clash with England, grabbing two wickets for 19 in 10 overs. The Kenyans too could not get him away, as his figures of 8-2-19-1 testified. Generating express speed, Bond bagged three West Indies wickets for 31. He was a handful for Bangladesh, conceding 15 runs in 10 overs and grabbing 2 wickets. More successes followed, two Irish wickets for 18 off 5 overs, two South African scalps for 26. He struck regularly and was rarely collared in the 2007 World Cup too. His 13 wickets in 7 matches, average of 16.38 and economy-rate of 3.05 tell an eloquent tale. Unfortunately, recurring injuries often kept one of the finest fast bowlers away from the arena.

Wickets 30, Ave 17.26, RO 3.50, Catches 6

John Davison

John Davison hit Canada's top score, lone century, highest aggregate, and took most wickets, in the World Cup. His batting strike-rate of 115.84 is second after Lance Klusener. He figures among the best allrounders. Davison struck the fastest World Cup hundred in just 67 balls, only bettered by one delivery by Matthew Hayden later. He equalled Brian Lara's record of fastest fifty off 23 balls in 2007, which was improved marginally by Brendon McCullum and Mark Boucher. Davison scored 71 per cent of his runs in boundaries, the best in the World Cup. In his early forays in 2003, Davison took a couple of Bangladesh wickets, and stretched Kenya with a splendid stint of 10-3-15-3. Earlier, he had displayed his batting prowess, hitting 31 off 32 balls. He blasted the West Indies attack for the quickest century, obliterating Clive Lloyd's 1975 record. The opening partnership realized 96 off 12 overs; Ishwar Maraj contributed 16. Davison raced to 111 off 76 balls with 8 fours and 6 sixes. He sizzled against New Zealand with 75 off 62 deliveries with 9 fours and 4 sixes, and bagged three wickets for 61. Captain in 2007, his best came against the Kiwis. He took two wickets for 67 and hit his quickfire 23-ball half-century. This scintillating batsman and off-spinner regaled as much as surprised.

Runs 307, Ave 34.11, SR 115.84, Catches 3
Wickets 12, Average 26.41, RO 4.46

RECORDS

RECORDS

TEAM PERFORMANCES

Countries	Played	Won	Lost	No Result	Success%	75	79	83	87	92	96	99	03	07
Australia	69	51	17	1 (tie)	74.63	RU	-	-	W	-	RU	W	W	W
South Africa	40	25	13	2 (ties)	65.00					SF	QF	SF	-	SF
West Indies	57	35	21	1	62.28	W	W	RU	-	-	SF	-	-	SE
England	59	36	22	1	61.86	SF	RU	SF	RU	RU	QF	-	-	SE
New Zealand	62	35	26	1	57.25	SF	SF	-	-	SF	QF	SF	SS	SF
India	58	32	25	1	56.03	-	-	W	SF	-	SF	SS	RU	-
Pakistan	56	30	24	2	55.35	-	SF	SF	SF	W	QF	RU	-	-
Sri Lanka	57	25	30	2 (1 tie)	45.61	-	-	-	-	-	W	-	SF	RU
Kenya	23	6	16	1*	28.26		-				-	-	SF	-
Ireland	9	2	6	1 (tie)	27.77									SE
Bangladesh	20	5	14	1	27.50									SE
Zimbabwe	45	8	33	4* (1 tie)	22.22			-	-	-	-	SS	SS	-
UAE	5	1	4	-	20.00						-			
Holland	14	2	12	-	14.28						-		-	-
Canada	12	1	11	-	8.33		-						-	-

Countries	Played	Won	Lost	No Result	Success%	75	79	83	87	92	96	99	03	07
East Africa	3	0	3	-	0.00	-								
Bermuda	3	0	3	-	0.00									-
Namibia	6	0	6	-	0.00								-	
Scotland	8	0	8	-	0.00							-		-

W–Winners, RU–Runners-up, SF–Semi-finals, QF–Quarter-finals, SS–Super-six, SE–Super-eight

The West Indies-Sri Lanka match scheduled for June 13, 1979 was abandoned without a ball being bowled. This match **has not** been included.

The following matches were forfeited:
In 1996: (i) By Australia against Sri Lanka, and (ii) By West Indies against Sri Lanka.
In 2003: (i) By England against Zimbabwe, and (ii) By New Zealand against Kenya.
These four matches **have not** been included.

* The match between Kenya and Zimbabwe on February 26, 1996 at Patna was washed out after 15.5 overs. This match **has** been included even though a new match was played the next day.

Records

MATCHES WON BY TEAMS BATTING FIRST / SECOND

	MATCHES WON		TIE / NO RESULT	TOTAL MATCHES
	BATTING FIRST	BATTING SECOND		
1975	8	7	-	15
1979	7	7	-	14
1983	15	12	-	27
1987	19	8	-	27
1992	18	19	2	39
1996	17	18	1	36
1999	19	21	2	42
2003	29	20	3	52
2007	25	25	1	51
TOTAL	157	137	9	303

The table shows that there is a distinct advantage batting first, but not a very significant advantage.

TEAM PERFORMANCES AFTER WINNING TOSS

	MATCHES	WON	LOST	BATTING FIRST		BATTING SECOND		TIE / NO RESULT
				Won	Lost	Won	Lost	
1975	15	7	8	3	3	4	5	-
1979	14	5	9	3	1	2	8	-
1983	27	14	13	8	6	6	7	-
1987	27	11	16	7	4	4	12	-
1992	39	23	14	10	6	13	8	2
1996	36	14	21	8	12	6	9	1
1999	42	17	23	5	9	12	14	2
2003	52	24	25	15	11	9	14	3
2007	51	24	26	8	9	16	17	1
TOTAL	303	139	155	67	61	72	94	9

The table indicates that more often than not, it is not an advantage to win the toss, and in fact teams often squander whatever advantage there is, by putting the opponents in to bat.

THE LEADING RUNGETTERS
(minimum 500 runs)

(* denotes not out)

Players	Countries	M	I	NO	HS	Runs	Ave	SR	100s	50s
Sachin Tendulkar	(India)	36	35	4	152	1796	57.93	88.21	4	13
Ricky Ponting	(Australia)	39	36	4	140*	1537	48.03	81.06	4	6
Brian Lara	(West Indies)	34	33	4	116	1225	42.24	86.26	2	7
Sanath Jayasuriya	(Sri Lanka)	38	37	3	120	1165	34.26	90.66	3	6
Adam Gilchrist	(Australia)	31	31	1	149	1085	36.16	98.01	1	8
Javed Miandad	(Pakistan)	33	30	5	103	1083	43.32	67.89	1	8
Stephen Fleming	(New Zealand)	33	33	3	134*	1075	35.83	76.89	2	5
Herschelle Gibbs	(South Africa)	25	23	4	143	1067	56.15	87.38	2	8
Aravinda de Silva	(Sri Lanka)	35	32	3	145	1064	36.68	86.57	2	6
Vivian Richards	(West Indies)	23	21	5	181	1013	63.31	85.05	3	5
Sourav Ganguly	(India)	21	21	3	183	1006	55.88	77.50	4	3
Mark Waugh	(Australia)	22	22	3	130	1004	52.84	83.04	4	4
Matthew Hayden	(Australia)	22	21	2	158	987	51.94	92.93	3	2
Steve Waugh	(Australia)	33	30	10	120*	978	48.90	81.02	1	6

Players	Countries	M	I	NO	HS	Runs	Ave	SR	100s	50s
Arjuna Ranatunga	(Sri Lanka)	30	29	8	88*	969	46.14	80.95	-	7
Jacques Kallis	(South Africa)	29	25	7	128*	923	51.27	74.79	1	7
Saeed Anwar	(Pakistan)	21	21	4	113*	915	53.82	79.08	3	3
Graham Gooch	(England)	21	21	1	115	897	44.85	63.81	1	8
Martin Crowe	(New Zealand)	21	21	5	100*	880	55.00	83.49	1	8
Rahul Dravid	(India)	22	21	7	145	860	61.42	74.97	2	6
Shivnaraine Chanderpaul	(West Indies)	26	24	3	102*	856	40.76	64.07	1	7
Desmond Haynes	(West Indies)	25	25	2	105	854	37.13	57.50	1	3
Mohammad Azharuddin	(India)	30	25	4	93	826	39.33	77.19	-	8
David Boon	(Australia)	16	16	1	100	815	54.33	73.75	2	5
Andy Flower	(Zimbabwe)	30	29	4	115*	815	32.60	68.25	1	4
Gary Kirsten	(South Africa)	21	21	4	188*	806	47.41	75.46	1	5
Scott Styris	(New Zealand)	181	6	5	141	767	69.72	89.08	2	5
Steve Tikolo	(Kenya)	23	22	1	96	724	34.47	69.48	-	8
Inzamam-ul-Haq	(Pakistan)	35	33	3	81	717	23.90	74.60	-	4
Rameez Raja	(Pakistan)	16	16	3	119*	700	53.84	64.22	3	2
Mahela Jayawardene	(Sri Lanka)	24	22	2	115*	671	33.55	83.04	1	4
Kapil Dev	(India)	26	24	6	175*	669	37.16	115.14	1	1

The leading rungetters (contd.)

Players	Countries	M	I	NO	HS	Runs	Ave	SR	100s	50s
Imran Khan	(Pakistan)	28	24	5	102*	666	35.05	65.61	1	4
Allan Lamb	(England)	19	17	4	102	656	50.46	84.10	1	3
Richie Richardson	(West Indies)	20	20	3	110	639	37.58	62.89	1	4
Graeme Hick	(England)	20	19	4	104*	635	42.33	74.00	1	6
Glenn Turner	(New Zealand)	14	14	4	171*	612	61.20	64.01	2	2
Alec Stewart	(England)	25	22	1	88	606	28.85	61.52	-	4
Aamir Sohail	(Pakistan)	16	16	-	114	598	37.37	69.29	2	4
Zaheer Abbas	(Pakistan)	14	14	2	103*	597	49.75	78.39	1	4
Roshan Mahanama	(Sri Lanka)	25	21	3	89	596	33.11	56.54	-	5
Gordon Greenidge	(West Indies)	15	15	2	106*	591	45.46	59.15	2	4
Salim Malik	(Pakistan)	27	23	5	100	591	32.83	82.65	1	4
Dean Jones	(Australia)	16	16	2	90	590	42.14	72.74	-	5
Ramnaresh Sarwan	(West Indies)	14	14	4	92	584	58.40	83.54	-	3
Geoff Marsh	(Australia)	13	13	1	126*	579	48.25	58.66	2	2
Andrew Hudson	(South Africa)	12	12	-	161	571	47.58	76.95	1	4
David Houghton	(Zimbabwe)	20	19	-	142	567	29.84	63.00	1	4
Chris Cairns	(New Zealand)	28	24	7	60	565	33.23	82.60	-	3
Graeme Smith	(South Africa)	13	13	1	91	564	47.00	99.82	-	6

Records

Players	Countries	M	I	NO	HS	Runs	Ave	SR	100s	50s
Sunil Gavaskar	(India)	19	19	3	103*	561	35.06	57.36	1	4
Michael Bevan	(Australia)	26	18	6	74*	537	44.75	64.38	-	5
Kumar Sangakkara	(Sri Lanka)	21	20	3	76	526	30.94	74.71	-	4
Ajay Jadeja	(India)	21	18	3	100*	522	34.80	71.40	1	2
Marvan Atapattu	(Sri Lanka)	15	15	3	124	521	43.41	79.29	2	3
Krishnamachari Srikkanth	(India)	23	23	1	75	521	23.68	68.28	-	2
Ijaz Ahmed	(Pakistan)	29	26	4	70	516	23.45	71.96	-	4
Andrew Symonds	(Australia)	18	13	8	143*	515	103.00	93.29	1	3
Grant Flower	(Zimbabwe)	21	20	2	78*	512	28.44	57.20	-	1
Craig McMillan	(New Zealand)	25	24	2	75	506	23.00	70.37	-	2
Ravindu Shah	(Kenya)	17	17	-	71	500	29.41	60.97	-	4

M-Matches, I-Innings, NO & *-Not Out, HS-Highest Score, Ave-Average, SR-Strike Rate

THE LEADING WICKET-TAKERS
(minimum 15 wickets)

Players	Countries	Balls	Mdns	Runs	Wkts	Ave	Best	RO
Glenn McGrath	(Australia)	1955	42	1292	71	18.19	7/15	3.96
Wasim Akram	(Pakistan)	1947	17	1311	55	23.83	5/28	4.04

The leading wicket-takers (contd.)

Players	Countries	Balls	Mdns	Runs	Wkts	Ave	Best	RO
Muttiah Muralitharan	(Sri Lanka)	1635	14	1044	53	19.69	4/19	3.83
Chaminda Vaas	(Sri Lanka)	1570	39	1040	49	21.22	6/25	3.97
Javagal Srinath	(India)	1700	21	1224	44	27.81	4/30	4.32
Allan Donald	(South Africa)	1313	14	913	38	24.02	4/17	4.17
Brad Hogg	(Australia)	951	10	654	34	19.23	4/27	4.12
Imran Khan	(Pakistan)	1017	18	655	34	19.26	4/37	3.86
Shane Warne	(Australia)	977	16	624	32	19.50	4/29	3.83
Chris Harris	(New Zealand)	1166	10	861	32	26.90	4/07	4.43
Anil Kumble	(India)	1039	5	708	31	22.83	4/32	4.08
Shaun Pollock	(South Africa)	1614	37	970	31	31.29	5/36	3.60
Shane Bond	(New Zealand)	886	21	518	30	17.26	6/23	3.50
Ian Botham	(England)	1332	33	762	30	25.40	4/31	3.43
Philip DeFreitas	(England)	1127	30	742	29	25.58	3/28	3.95
Kapil Dev	(India)	1422	27	892	28	31.85	5/43	3.76
Courtney Walsh	(West Indies)	948	23	547	27	20.25	4/25	3.46
Craig McDermott	(Australia)	894	8	599	27	22.18	5/44	4.02
Shoaib Akhtar	(Pakistan)	749	8	643	27	23.81	4/46	5.15
Steve Waugh	(Australia)	1039	7	814	27	30.14	3/36	4.70

Players	Countries	Balls	Mdns	Runs	Wkts	Ave	Best	RO
Sanath Jayasuriya	(Sri Lanka)	1315	4	1060	27	39.25	3/12	4.83
Mushtaq Ahmed	(Pakistan)	810	5	549	26	21.11	3/16	4.06
Andy Roberts	(West Indies)	1021	29	552	26	21.23	3/32	3.24
Damien Fleming	(Australia)	800	12	583	26	22.42	5/36	4.37
Curtly Ambrose	(West Indies)	987	20	499	24	20.79	3/28	3.03
Abdul Qadir	(Pakistan)	814	8	506	24	21.08	5/44	3.72
Jacob Oram	(New Zealand)	795	15	547	24	22.79	4/52	4.12
Manoj Prabhakar	(India)	871	10	640	24	26.66	4/19	4.40
Shaun Tait	(Australia)	507	1	467	23	20.30	4/39	5.52
Saqlain Mushtaq	(Pakistan)	674	7	494	23	21.47	5/35	4.39
Zaheer Khan	(India)	704	8	496	23	21.56	4/42	4.22
Andrew Flintoff	(England)	814	12	534	23	23.21	4/43	3.93
Brett Lee	(Australia)	499	9	394	22	17.90	5/42	4.73
Richard Hadlee	(New Zealand)	877	38	421	22	19.13	5/25	2.88
Madan Lal	(India)	698	12	426	22	19.36	4/20	3.66
Waqar Younis	(Pakistan)	559	8	466	22	21.18	4/26	5.00
Lance Klusener	(South Africa)	605	7	487	22	22.13	5/21	4.82
Heath Streak	(Zimbabwe)	1050	13	804	22	36.54	3/35	4.59

The leading wicket-takers (contd.)

Players	Countries	Balls	Mdns	Runs	Wkts	Ave	Best	RO
Geoff Allott	(New Zealand)	526	7	325	20	16.25	4/37	3.70
Michael Holding	(West Indies)	695	16	341	20	17.05	4/33	2.94
Thomas Odoyo	(Kenya)	864	9	683	20	34.15	4/28	4.74
Roger Binny	(India)	570	9	382	19	20.10	4/29	4.02
Andrew Hall	(South Africa)	594	8	438	19	23.05	5/18	4.42
Willie Watson	(New Zealand)	792	14	571	19	30.05	3/37	4.32
Lasith Malinga	(Sri Lanka)	350	6	284	18	15.77	4/54	4.86
Bob Willis	(England)	709	27	315	18	17.50	4/11	2.66
Asantha de Mel	(Sri Lanka)	542	13	449	18	24.94	5/32	4.97
Roger Harper	(West Indies)	792	10	488	18	27.11	4/47	3.69
Aaqib Javed	(Pakistan)	746	13	517	18	28.72	3/21	4.15
James Anderson	(England)	720	7	554	18	30.77	4/25	4.61
Maurice Odumbe	(Kenya)	701	9	567	18	31.50	4/38	4.85
Gavin Larsen	(New Zealand)	1020	12	599	18	33.27	3/16	3.52
Carl Hooper	(West Indies)	924	3	659	18	36.61	3/42	4.27
Daniel Vettori	(New Zealand)	976	3	706	18	39.22	4/23	4.34
Chris Cairns	(New Zealand)	880	9	755	18	41.94	3/19	5.14
Brian McMillan	(South Africa)	696	12	433	17	25.47	3/11	3.73

Players	Countries	Balls	Mdns	Runs	Wkts	Ave	Best	RO
Venkatesh Prasad	(India)	779	5	578	17	34.00	5/27	4.45
Andy Bichel	(Australia)	342	7	197	16	12.31	7/20	3.45
Vasbert Drakes	(West Indies)	311	7	208	16	13.00	5/33	4.01
Chris Old	(England)	543	18	243	16	15.18	4/08	2.68
Nathan Bracken	(Australia)	430	10	258	16	16.12	4/19	3.60
Mohinder Amarnath	(India)	663	9	431	16	26.93	3/12	3.90
Sarfraz Nawaz	(Pakistan)	714	15	435	16	27.18	4/44	3.65
Makhaya Ntini	(South Africa)	691	10	469	16	29.31	4/24	4.07
Pramodaya Wikremasinghe	(Sri Lanka)	817	8	625	16	39.06	3/30	4.58
Eddo Brandes	(Zimbabwe)	775	11	641	16	40.06	4/21	4.96
Aravinda de Silva	(Sri Lanka)	810	2	671	16	41.93	3/42	4.97
John Traicos	(Zimbabwe)	1128	13	673	16	42.06	3/35	3.57
Jacques Kallis	(South Africa)	1086	10	781	16	48.81	3/26	4.31
Patrick Patterson	(West Indies)	396	2	278	15	18.53	3/31	4.21
Ashish Nehra	(India)	415	9	289	15	19.26	6/23	4.17
Paul Strang	(Zimbabwe)	520	6	388	15	25.86	5/21	4.47
Darren Gough	(England)	598	8	430	15	28.66	4/34	4.31

Mdns–Maidens, Wkts–Wickets, Ave–Average, RO–Runs per over

THE LEADING ALLROUNDERS
(minimum 300 runs & 12 wickets)

Players	Countries	M	Runs	Ave	SR	Wkts	Ave	RO	Quotient
Lance Klusener	(South Africa)	14	372	124.00	121.17	22	22.13	4.82	5.60
Neil Johnson	(Zimbabwe)	8	367	52.42	73.99	12	19.41	4.66	2.70
Scott Styris	(New Zealand)	18	767	69.72	89.08	13	32.69	4.63	2.13
Imran Khan	(Pakistan)	28	666	35.05	65.61	34	19.26	3.86	1.81
Steve Waugh	(Australia)	33	978	48.90	81.02	27	30.14	4.70	1.62
John Davison	(Canada)	9	307	34.11	115.84	12	26.41	4.46	1.29
Steve Tikolo	(Kenya)	23	724	34.47	69.48	14	28.21	5.30	1.22
Kapil Dev	(India)	26	669	37.16	115.14	28	31.85	3.76	1.16
Chris Harris	(New Zealand)	28	431	28.73	68.84	32	26.90	4.43	1.06
Jacques Kallis	(South Africa)	29	923	51.27	74.79	16	48.81	4.31	1.05
Maurice Odumbe	(Kenya)	19	452	30.13	73.13	18	31.50	4.85	0.95
Tom Moody	(Australia)	18	329	29.90	73.27	14	32.85	4.50	0.91
Sanath Jayasuriya	(Sri Lanka)	38	1165	34.26	90.66	27	39.25	4.83	0.87
Aravinda de Silva	(Sri Lanka)	35	1064	36.68	86.57	16	41.93	4.97	0.87
Wasim Akram	(Pakistan)	38	426	19.36	100.70	55	23.83	4.04	0.81
Heath Streak	(Zimbabwe)	22	328	29.81	73.37	22	36.54	4.59	0.81

Players	Countries	M	Runs	Ave	SR	Wkts	Ave	RO	Quotient
Chris Cairns	(New Zealand)	28	565	33.23	82.60	18	41.94	5.14	0.79
Thomas Odoyo	(Kenya)	20	361	25.78	67.22	20	34.14	4.74	0.75

THE LEADING WICKETKEEPER-BATSMEN
(minimum 250 runs & 15 dismissals)

Players	Countries	Matches	Runs	Ave	SR	Ct	St
Adam Gilchrist	(Australia)	31	1085	36.16	98.01	45	7
Kumar Sangakkara	(Sri Lanka)	21	526	30.94	74.71	26	6
Mark Boucher	(South Africa)	25	381	27.21	94.07	31	-
Moin Khan	(Pakistan)	20	286	28.60	106.31	23	7
Alec Stewart	(England)	20	520	32.50	66.49	21	2
Ridley Jacobs	(West Indies)	11	270	67.50	54.00	21	1
Rahul Dravid	(India)	12	463	77.16	74.08	15	1
Kennedy Otieno	(Kenya)	15	401	26.73	54.70	11	4

Note: In the instances of Stewart, Dravid and Otieno, statistics of only those matches have been taken in which they kept wickets. The other five kept wickets in all the matches that they played. David Houghton bagged 14 catches and 2 stumpings, but 4 of the catches were as a fielder in 1992. Andy Flower effected 12 catches and 3 stumpings, but one of the catches was as a fielder in 2003.

Records

TEAMS

HIGHEST TOTALS

413 for 5 (50 overs)	India v Bermuda	Port of Spain	2007
398 for 5 (50 overs)	Sri Lanka v Kenya	Kandy	1996
377 for 6 (50 overs)	Australia v South Africa	Basseterre, St. Kitts	2007
373 for 6 (50 overs)	India v Sri Lanka	Taunton	1999
363 for 5 (50 overs)	New Zealand v Canada	Gros Islet, St. Lucia	2007
360 for 4 (50 overs)	West Indies v Sri Lanka	Karachi	1987
359 for 2 (50 overs)	Australia v India	Johannesburg	2003
358 for 5 (50 overs)	Australia v Holland	Basseterre, St. Kitts	2007
356 for 4 (50 overs)	South Africa v West Indies	St. George's, Grenada	2007
353 for 7 (40 overs)	South Africa v Holland	Basseterre, St. Kitts	2007

HIGHEST TOTALS FOR THE OTHER TEAMS

349 (49.5 overs)	Pakistan v Zimbabwe	Kingston	2007
340 for 2 (50 overs)	Zimbabwe v Namibia	Harare	2003

334 for 4 (60 overs)	England v India	Lord's	1975
314 for 4 (50 overs)	Holland v Namibia	Bloemfontein	2003
254 for 7 (50 overs)	Kenya v Sri Lanka	Kandy	1996
251 for 8 (50 overs)	Bangladesh v South Africa	Providence, Guyana	2007
250 (46.5 overs)	Namibia v Holland	Bloemfontein	2003
249 (49.2 overs)	Canada v New Zealand	Gros Islet, St. Lucia	2007
243 for 7 (50 overs)	Ireland v Bangladesh	Bridgetown	2007
220 for 3 (44.2 overs)	United Arab Emirates v Holland	Lahore	1996
186 for 8 (50 overs)	Scotland v South Africa	Basseterre, St. Kitts	2007
156 (43.1 overs)	Bermuda v India	Port of Spain	2007
128 for 8 (60 overs)	East Africa v New Zealand	Birmingham	1975

HIGHEST TOTALS : BATTING SECOND

313 for 7 (49.2 overs)	Sri Lanka v Zimbabwe	New Plymouth	1992
301 for 9 (49.5 overs)	England v West Indies	Bridgetown	2007

HIGHEST TOTAL IN FINAL

359 for 2 (50 overs)	Australia v India	Johannesburg	2003

Records

HIGHEST MATCH AGGREGATES

671 for 16 wickets (98 overs)	Australia v South Africa	Basseterre, St. Kitts	2007
652 for 12 wickets (100 overs)	Sri Lanka v Kenya	Kandy	1996

LOWEST TOTALS

36 (18.4 overs)	Canada v Sri Lanka	Paarl	2003
45 (40.3 overs)	Canada v England	Manchester	1979
45 (14 overs)	Namibia v Australia	Potchefstroom	2003
68 (31.3 overs)	Scotland v West Indies	Leicester	1999
74 (40.2 overs)	Pakistan v England	Adelaide	1992
77 (27.4 overs)	Ireland v Sri Lanka	St. George's, Grenada	2007
78 (24.4 overs)	Bermuda v Sri Lanka	Port of Spain	2007
84 (17.4 overs)	Namibia v Pakistan	Kimberley	2003
86 (37.2 overs)	Sri Lanka v West Indies	Manchester	1975
91 (30 overs)	Ireland v Australia	Bridgetown	2007
93 (36.2 overs)	England v Australia	Leeds	1975
93 (35.2 overs)	West Indies v Kenya	Pune	1996
94 (52.3 overs)	East Africa v England	Birmingham	1975

99 (19.1 overs)	Zimbabwe v Pakistan	Kingston	2007

LOWEST TOTALS FOR THE OTHER TEAMS

104 (35.5 overs)	Kenya v West Indies	Kimberley	2003
108 (35.1 overs)	Bangladesh v South Africa	Bloemfontein	2003
112 (30.1 overs)	New Zealand v Australia	Port Elizabeth	2003
122 (30.2 overs)	Holland v Australia	Potchefstroom	2003
125 (41.4 overs)	India v Australia	Centurion	2003
129 (38.2 overs)	Australia v India	Chelmsford	1983
136 (48.3 overs)	United Arab Emirates v England	Peshawar	1996
184 (48.4 overs)	South Africa v Bangladesh	Providence, Guyana	2007

LOWEST TOTAL IN FINAL

132 (39 overs)	Pakistan v Australia	Lord's	1999

LOWEST WINNING TOTALS BATTING FIRST (COMPLETED INNINGS)

134 (46.1 overs)	Zimbabwe v England	Albury	1992
165 for 9 (60 overs)	England v Pakistan	Leeds	1979

Records

Lowest winning totals batting first (contd.)

166 (49.3 overs)	Kenya v West Indies	Pune	1996
180 (49.1 overs)	Canada v Bangladesh	Durban	2003
183 (54.4 overs)	India v West Indies	Lord's	1983
185 (50 overs)	Bangladesh v Scotland	Edinburgh	1999
199 for 9 (50 overs)	South Africa v Sri Lanka	Northampton	1999

LOWEST MATCH AGGREGATES

73 for 11 wickets (23.2 overs)	Canada v Sri Lanka	Paarl	2003
91 for 12 wickets (54.2 overs)	Canada v England	Manchester	1979

LARGEST MARGINS OF VICTORY (by runs)

257 runs	India beat Bermuda	Port of Spain	2007
256 runs	Australia beat Namibia	Potchefstroom	2003
243 runs	Sri Lanka beat Bermuda	Port of Spain	2007
229 runs	Australia beat Holland	Basseterre, St. Kitts	2007
221 runs	South Africa beat Holland	Basseterre, St. Kitts	2007
215 runs	Australia beat New Zealand	St. George's, Grenada	2007

| 203 runs | Australia beat Scotland | Basseterre, St. Kitts | 2007 |
| 202 runs | England beat India | Lord's | 1975 |

LARGEST MARGINS OF VICTORY (by wickets)

10 wickets	India beat East Africa	Leeds	1975
10 wickets	West Indies beat Zimbabwe	Birmingham	1983
10 wickets	West Indies beat Pakistan	Melbourne	1992
10 wickets	South Africa beat Kenya	Potchefstroom	2003
10 wickets	Sri Lanka beat Bangladesh	Pietermaritzburg	2003
10 wickets	South Africa beat Bangladesh	Bloemfontein	2003
10 wickets	Australia beat Bangladesh	North Sound, Antigua	2007

BEST WINNING SEQUENCE

23 wins	Australia (20.6.1999 to 28.4.2007)
9 wins	West Indies (7.6.1975 to 23.6.1979)
8 wins	India (19.2.2003 to 20.3.2003)
7 wins	New Zealand (22.2.1992 to 15.3.1992)
7 wins	Pakistan (11.3.1992 to 26.2.1996)

BEST SEQUENCE WITHOUT DEFEAT

29 matches	Australia (27.5.1999 to 28.4.2007)

NARROWEST MARGINS OF VICTORY (by runs)

1 run	Australia beat India	Madras	1987
1 run	Australia beat India	Brisbane	1992
2 runs	Sri Lanka beat England	North Sound, Antigua	2007
3 runs	New Zealand beat Zimbabwe	Hyderabad (Ind)	1987
3 runs	Australia beat New Zealand	Indore	1987
3 runs	Zimbabwe beat India	Leicester	1999
3 runs	West Indies beat South Africa	Cape Town	2003

NARROWEST MARGINS OF VICTORY (by wickets)

1 wicket	West Indies beat Pakistan	Birmingham	1975
1 wicket	Pakistan beat West Indies	Lahore	1987
1 wicket	South Africa beat Sri Lanka	Providence, Guyana	2007
1 wicket	England beat West Indies	Bridgetown	2007

TIE

Australia 213 (49.2 overs), South Africa 213 (49.4 overs)	Semi-final, Birmingham	1999
Sri Lanka 268 for 9 (50 overs), South Africa 229 for 6 (45 overs)	D-L Method Durban	2003
Ireland 221 for 9 (50 overs), Zimbabwe 221 (50 overs)	Kingston	2007

MOST CONSECUTIVE MATCHES WITHOUT A VICTORY

18	Zimbabwe	(11.6.1983 to 14.3.1992)
10	Holland	(17.2.1996 to 28.2.2003)
8	Scotland	(16.5.1999 to 22.3.2007)
8	Canada	(15.2.2003 to 22.3.2007)

NO RESULTS

India v Sri Lanka	Mackay	1992
England v Pakistan	Adelaide	1992
New Zealand v Zimbabwe	Leeds	1999
Bangladesh v West Indies	Benoni	2003
Pakistan v Zimbabwe	Bulawayo	2003

Records

MATCH REPLAYED

Kenya v Zimbabwe	Patna	1996

MATCHES NOT PLAYED

Sri Lanka v West Indies (washed out)	The Oval	1979
Sri Lanka v Australia (forfeited by Australia)	Colombo (Premadasa)	1996
Sri Lanka v West Indies (forfeited by West Indies)	Colombo (SSC)	1996
Zimbabwe v England (forfeited by England)	Harare	2003
Kenya v New Zealand (forfeited by New Zealand)	Nairobi	2003

MOST EXTRAS CONCEDED BY A TEAM IN AN INNINGS

59	Scotland v Pakistan	Chester-Le-Street	1999
51	India v Zimbabwe	Leicester	1999

MOST EXTRAS CONCEDED IN A MATCH

96	Pakistan (37) v Scotland (59)	Chester-Le-Street	1999
90	India (51) v Zimbabwe (39)	Leicester	1999

BATTING

HIGHEST INDIVIDUAL SCORES

188* (159)	Gary Kirsten	South Africa v UAE	Rawalpindi	1996
183 (158)	Sourav Ganguly	India v Sri Lanka	Taunton	1999
181 (125)	Vivian Richards	West Indies v Sri Lanka	Karachi	1987
175* (138)	Kapil Dev	India v Zimbabwe	Tunbridge Wells	1983
172* (151)	Craig Wishart	Zimbabwe v Namibia	Harare	2003
171* (201)	Glenn Turner	New Zealand v East Africa	Birmingham	1975
160 (121)	Imran Nazir	Pakistan v Zimbabwe	Kingston	2007
158 (143)	Matthew Hayden	Australia v West indies	North Sound	2007
161 (132)	Andrew Hudson	South Africa v Holland	Rawalpindi	1996
152 (151)	Sachin Tendulkar	India v Namibia	Pietermaritzburg	2003

HIGHEST INDIVIDUAL SCORES FOR THE OTHER COUNTRIES

145 (115)	Aravinda de Silva	Sri Lanka v Kenya	Kandy	1996
137 (147)	Dennis Amiss	England v India	Lord's	1975
134* (129)	Klaas van Noortwijk	Holland v Namibia	Bloemfontein	2003

Highest individual scores for the other countries (contd.)

115* (137)	Jeremy Bray	Ireland v Zimbabwe	Kingston	2007
111 (76)	John Davison	Canada v West Indies	Centurion	2003
96 (95)	Steve Tikolo	Kenya v Sri Lanka	Kandy	1996
87 (83)	Mohammad Ashraful	Bangladesh v South Africa	Providence	2007
85 (86)	Jan Berrie Burger	Namibia v England	Port Elizabeth	2003
84 (68)	Salim Raza	UAE v Holland	Lahore	1996
76* (105)	David Hemp	Bermuda v India	Port of Spain	2007
76 (111)	Gavin Hamilton	Scotland v Pakistan	Chester-Le-Street	1999
45 (123)	Frasat Ali	East Africa v New Zealand	Birmingham	1975

(In brackets: Balls faced)

HUNDREDS IN THE OPENING MATCH OF EACH WORLD CUP

1975	Glenn Turner	171*	New Zealand v East Africa	Birmingham
	Dennis Amiss	137	England v India	Lord's
1979	Gordon Greenidge	106*	West Indies v India	Birmingham
1983	Allan Lamb	102	England v New Zealand	The Oval
1987	Javed Miandad	103	Pakistan v Sri Lanka	Hyderabad (Pak)

1992	Martin Crowe	100*	New Zealand v Australia	Auckland
	David Boon	100	Australia v New Zealand	Auckland
1996	Nathan Astle	101	New Zealand v England	Ahmedabad
1999	For the first time a century was not scored in the opening match			
2003	Brian Lara	116	West Indies v South Africa	Cape Town
2007	No century was scored in the opening match			

CENTURIES ON WORLD CUP DEBUT

Glenn Turner	171*	New Zealand v East Africa	Birmingham	1975
Dennis Amiss	137	England v India	Lord's	1975
Allan Lamb	102	England v New Zealand	The Oval	1983
Trevor Chappell	110	Australia v India	Nottingham	1983
Geoff Marsh	110	Australia v India	Madras	1987
Andy Flower	115*	Zimbabwe v Sri Lanka	New Plymouth	1992
Nathan Astle	101	New Zealand v England	Ahmedabad	1996
Gary Kirsten	188*	South Africa v UAE	Rawalpindi	1996
Craig Wishart	172*	Zimbabwe v Namibia	Harare	2003
Scott Styris	141	New Zealand v Sri Lanka	Bloemfontein	2003

Centuries on World Cup debut (contd.)

Andrew Symonds	143*	Australia v Pakistan	Johannesburg	2003
Jeremy Bray	115*	Ireland v Zimbabwe	Kingston	2007

MORE THAN ONE HUNDRED

Mark Waugh (Australia)	(4)			
	130	v Kenya	Visakhapatnam	1996
	126	v India	Mumbai	1996
	110	v New Zealand	Madras	1996
	104	v Zimbabwe	Lord's	1999
Sachin Tendulkar (India)	(4)			
	127*	v Kenya	Cuttack	1996
	137	v Sri Lanka	New Delhi	1996
	140*	v Kenya	Bristol	1999
	152	v Namibia	Pietermaritzburg	2003
Sourav Ganguly (India)	(4)			
	183	v Sri Lanka	Taunton	1999
	112*	v Namibia	Pietermaritzburg	2003
	107*	v Kenya	Cape Town	2003
	111*	v Kenya	Durban	2003
Ricky Ponting (Australia)	(4)			
	102	v West Indies	Jaipur	1996
	114	v Sri Lanka	Centurion	2003
	140*	v India	Johannesburg	2003
	113	v Scotland	Basseterre	2007

Vivian Richards (West Indies)	(3)	138*	v England	Lord's	1979
		119	v India	The Oval	1983
		181	v Sri Lanka	Karachi	1987
Rameez Raja (Pakistan)	(3)	113	v England	Karachi	1987
		102*	v West Indies	Melbourne	1992
		119*	v New Zealand	Christchurch	1992
Saeed Anwar (Pakistan)	(3)	103	v Zimbabwe	The Oval	1999
		113*	v New Zealand	Manchester	1999
		101	v India	Centurion	2003
Sanath Jayasuriya (Sri Lanka)	(3)	120	v New Zealand	Bloemfontein	2003
		109	v Bangladesh	Port of Spain	2007
		115	v West Indies	Providence	2007
Matthew Hayden (Australia)	(3)	101	v South Africa	Basseterre	2007
		158	v West Indies	North Sound	2007
		103	v New Zealand	St. George's	2007
Glenn Turner (New Zealand)	(2)	171*	v East Africa	Birmingham	1975
		114*	v India	Manchester	1975
Gordon Greenidge (West Indies)	(2)	106*	v India	Birmingham	1979
		105*	v Zimbabwe	Worcester	1983

More than one hundred (contd.)

Geoff Marsh (Australia)	(2)	110	v India	Madras	1987
		126*	v New Zealand	Chandigarh	1987
David Boon (Australia)	(2)	100	v New Zealand	Auckland	1992
		100	v West Indies	Melbourne	1992
Aamir Sohail (Pakistan)	(2)	114	v Zimbabwe	Hobart	1992
		111	v South Africa	Karachi	1996
Nathan Astle (New Zealand)	(2)	101	v England	Ahmedabad	1996
		102*	v Zimbabwe	Bloemfontein	2003
Aravinda de Silva (Sri Lanka)	(2)	145	v Kenya	Kandy	1996
		107*	v Australia	Lahore	1996
Brian Lara (West Indies)	(2)	111	v South Africa	Karachi	1996
		116	v South Africa	Cape Town	2003
Rahul Dravid (India)	(2)	104*	v Kenya	Bristol	1999
		145	v Sri Lanka	Taunton	1999
Herschelle Gibbs (South Africa)	(2)	101	v Australia	Leeds	1999
		143	v New Zealand	Johannesburg	2003
Marvan Atapattu (Sri Lanka)	(2)	124	v South Africa	Durban	2003
		103*	v Zimbabwe	East London	2003

Scott Styris (New Zealand)	(2)	141	v Sri Lanka	Bloemfontein	2003
		111*	v New Zealand	St. George's	2007
Stephen Fleming (New Zealand)	(2)	134*	v South Africa	Johannesburg	2003
		102*	v Bangladesh	North Sound	2007
Kevin Pietersen (England)	(2)	104	v Australia	North Sound	2007
		100	v West Indies	Bridgetown	2007

~ Mark Waugh, Sourav Ganguly and Matthew Hayden are the only players to score three centuries in a single World Cup

ONE HUNDRED

Dennis Amiss (England)	137	v India	Lord's	1975
Keith Fletcher (England)	131	v New Zealand	Nottingham	1975
Alan Turner (Australia)	101	v Sri Lanka	The Oval	1975
Clive Lloyd (West Indies)	102	v Australia	Lord's	1975
Allan Lamb (England)	102	v New Zealand	The Oval	1983
David Gower (England)	130	v Sri Lanka	Taunton	1983
Trevor Chappell (Australia)	110	v India	Nottingham	1983
Imran Khan (Pakistan)	102*	v Sri Lanka	Leeds	1983
Kapil Dev (India)	175*	v Zimbabwe	Tunbridge Wells	1983

One hundred (contd.)

Zaheer Abbas (Pakistan)	103*	v New Zealand	Nottingham	1983
Javed Miandad (Pakistan)	103	v Sri Lanka	Hyderabad (Pak)	1987
David Houghton (Zimbabwe)	142	v New Zealand	Hyderabad (Ind)	1987
Desmond Haynes (West Indies)	105	v Sri Lanka	Karachi	1987
Salim Malik (Pakistan)	100	v Sri Lanka	Faisalabad	1987
Richie Richardson (West Indies)	110	v Pakistan	Karachi	1987
Sunil Gavaskar (India)	103*	v New Zealand	Nagpur	1987
Graham Gooch (England)	115	v India	Bombay	1987
Martin Crowe (New Zealand)	100*	v Australia	Auckland	1992
Andy Flower (Zimbabwe)	115*	v Sri Lanka	New Plymouth	1992
Phil Simmons (West Indies)	110	v Sri Lanka	Berri	1992
Gary Kirsten (South Africa)	188*	v UAE	Rawalpindi	1996
Graeme Hick (England)	104*	v Holland	Peshawar	1996
Andrew Hudson (South Africa)	161	v Holland	Rawalpindi	1996
Vinod Kambli (India)	106	v Zimbabwe	Kanpur	1996
Chris Harris (New Zealand)	130	v Australia	Madras	1996
Ajay Jadeja (India)	100*	v Australia	The Oval	1999
Neil Johnson (Zimbabwe)	132*	v Australia	Lord's	1999

Player	Score	Opponent	Venue	Year
Steve Waugh (Australia)	120*	v South Africa	Leeds	1999
Craig Wishart (Zimbabwe)	172*	v Namibia	Harare	2003
Andrew Symonds (Australia)	143*	v Pakistan	Johannesburg	2003
John Davison (Canada)	111	v West Indies	Centurion	2003
Feiko Kloppenburg (Holland)	121	v Namibia	Bloemfontein	2003
Klaas van Noortwijk (Holland)	134*	v Namibia	Bloemfontein	2003
Chris Gayle (West Indies)	119	v Kenya	Kimberley	2003
Jeremy Bray (Ireland)	115*	v Zimbabwe	Kingston	2007
Jacques Kallis (South Africa)	128*	v Holland	Basseterre	2007
Brad Hodge (Australia)	123	v Holland	Basseterre	2007
Virender Sehwag (India)	114	v Bermuda	Port of Spain	2007
Imran Nazir (Pakistan)	160	v Zimbabwe	Kingston	2007
Lou Vincent (New Zealand)	101	v Canada	Gros Islet	2007
Shivnaraine Chanderpaul (West Indies)	102*	v Ireland	Kingston	2007
Abraham de Villiers (South Africa)	146	v West Indies	St. George's	2007
Mahela Jayawardene (Sri Lanka)	115*	v New Zealand	Kingston	2007
Adam Gilchrist (Australia)	149	v Sri Lanka	Bridgetown	2007

~ A total of 103 hundreds have been scored by 67 players

YOUNGEST CENTURIONS

Ricky Ponting (Australia)	21 years 76 days	102 v West Indies	1996
Sachin Tendulkar (India)	22 years 300 days	127* v Kenya	1996
Andy Flower (Zimbabwe)	23 years 301 days	115* v Sri Lanka	1992

HUNDREDS IN CONSECUTIVE MATCHES

Mark Waugh (Australia)	130 v Kenya, Visakhapatnam	& 126 v India	Mumbai	1996
Rahul Dravid (India)	104* v Kenya, Bristol	& 145 v Sri Lanka	Taunton	1999
Saeed Anwar (Pakistan)	103 v Zimbabwe, The Oval	& 113* v New Zealand	Manchester	1999
Ricky Ponting (Australia)	140* v India, Johannesburg, 2003	& 113 v Scotland	Basseterre	2007
Matthew Hayden (Australia)	101 v South Africa, Basseterre	& 158 v West Indies	North Sound	2007

TWO SEPARATE HUNDREDS IN THE SAME INNINGS

Desmond Haynes (105)	&	Vivian Richards (181)	West Indies v Sri Lanka	Karachi	1987
Rahul Dravid (104*)	&	Sachin Tendulkar (140*)	India v Kenya	Bristol	1999
Sourav Ganguly (183)	&	Rahul Dravid (145)	India v Sri Lanka	Taunton	1999
Sachin Tendulkar (152)	&	Sourav Ganguly (112*)	Namibia	Pietermaritzburg	2003
Feiko Kloppenburg (121)	&	Klaas van Noortwijk (134*)	Holland v Namibia	Bloemfontein	2003

TOP STRIKE RATES – RUNS PER 100 BALLS FACED (minimum 300 runs)

	M	I	NO	HS	Runs	Ave	100s	50s	S/R
Lance Klusener (South Africa)	14	11	8	57	372	124.00	-	3	121.17
John Davison (Canada)	9	9	-	111	307	34.11	1	2	115.84
Kapil Dev (India)	26	24	6	175*	669	37.16	1	1	115.14
Abraham de Villiers (South Africa)	10	10	-	146	372	37.20	1	2	100.81
Wasim Akram (Pakistan)	38	30	8	43	426	19.36	-	-	100.70
Graeme Smith (Australia)	13	13	1	91	564	47.00	-	6	99.82
Adam Gilchrist (Australia)	31	31	1	149	1085	36.16	1	8	98.01
Virender Sehwag (India)	14	14	-	114	463	33.07	1	2	95.66
Michael Clarke (Australla)	11	9	4	93*	436	87.20	-	4	94.98
Yuvraj Singh (India)	14	13	3	83	376	37.60	-	3	94.71
Mark Boucher (South Africa)	25	19	5	75*	381	27.21	-	2	94.07
Andrew Symonds (Australla)	18	13	8	143*	515	103.00	1	3	93.29
Matthew Hayden (Australla)	22	21	2	158	987	51.94	3	2	92.93
Sanath Jayasuriya (Sri Lanka)	38	37	3	120	1165	34.26	3	6	90.66
Scott Styris (New Zealand)	18	16	5	141	767	69.72	2	5	89.08
Sachin Tendulkar (India)	36	35	4	152	1796	57.93	4	13	88.21

Top strike rates (contd.)

	M	I	NO	HS	Runs	Ave	100s	50s	S/R
Jonty Rhodes (South Africa)	24	20	3	43	354	20.82	-	-	88.05
Mark Greatbatch (New Zealand)	7	7	-	73	313	44.71	-	3	87.92
Herschelle Gibbs (South Africa)	25	23	4	143	1067	56.15	2	8	87.38
Mike Gatting (England)	15	13	2	60	437	39.72	-	3	87.05
Aravinda de Silva (Sri Lanka)	35	32	3	145	1064	36.68	2	6	86.57
Brian Lara (West Indies)	34	33	4	116	1225	42.24	2	7	86.26
Vivian Richards (West Indies)	23	21	5	181	1013	63.31	3	5	85.05
Clive Lloyd (West Indies)	17	11	2	102	393	43.66	1	2	84.88
Allan Lamb (England)	19	17	4	102	656	50.46	1	3	84.10
Ramnaresh Sarwan (West Indies)	14	14	4	92	584	58.40	-	3	83.54
Martin Crowe (New Zealand)	21	21	5	100*	880	55.00	1	8	83.49
Mark Waugh (Australia)	22	22	3	130	1004	52.84	4	4	83.04
Mahela Jayawardene (Sri Lanka)	24	22	2	115*	671	33.55	1	4	83.04
Salim Malik (Pakistan)	27	23	5	100	591	32.83	1	4	82.65
Chris Cairns (New Zealand)	28	24	7	60	565	33.23	-	3	82.60
David Gower (England)	12	11	3	130	434	54.25	1	1	82.35
Darren Lehmann (Australia)	19	16	5	76	360	32.72	-	3	81.08

	M	I	NO	HS	Runs	Ave	100s	50s	S/R
Ricky Ponting (Australia)	39	36	4	140*	1537	48.03	4	6	81.06
Steve Waugh (Australia)	33	30	10	120*	978	48.90	1	6	81.02
Kevin Pietersen (England)	9	9	1	104	444	55.50	2	3	81.02
Arjuna Ranatunga (Sri Lanka)	30	29	8	88*	969	46.14	-	7	80.95
Hansie Cronje (South Africa)	23	20	4	78	476	29.75	-	2	80.67
Damien Martyn (Australia)	12	10	3	88*	352	50.28	-	4	80.00

FASTEST HUNDRED

66 Balls	Matthew Hayden	Australia v South Africa	Basseterre	2007
67 Balls	John Davison	Canada v West Indies	Centurion	2003
72 Balls	Adam Gilchrist	Australia v Sri Lanka	Bridgetown	2007
81 Balls	Virender Sehwag	India v Bermuda	Port of Spain	2007
82 Balls	Clive Lloyd	West Indies v Australia	Lord's	1975
82 Balls	Brad Hodge	Australia v Holland	Basseterre	2007
83 Balls	Brian Lara	West Indies v South Africa	Karachi	1996
84 Balls	Sachin Tendulkar	India v Kenya	Bristol	1999
85 Balls	Sunil Gavaskar	India v New Zealand	Nagpur	1987
85 Balls	Ricky Ponting	Australia v Scotland	Basseterre	2007
85 Balls	Sanath Jayasuriya	Sri Lanka v Bangladesh	Port of Spain	2007

Records

FASTEST FIFTY

20 Balls	Brendon McCullum	New Zealand v Canada	Gros Islet	2007
21 Balls	Mark Boucher	South Africa v Holland	Basseterre	2007
22 Balls	Mark Boucher	South Africa v West Indies	St George's	2007
23 Balls	Brian Lara	West Indies v Canada	Centurion	2003
23 Balls	John Davison	Canada v New Zealand	Gros Islet	2007
24 Balls	Wavell Hinds	West Indies v Canada	Centurion	2003
25 Balls	Andy Blignaut	Zimbabwe v Australia	Bulawayo	2003
25 Balls	John Davison	Canada v New Zealand	Benoni	2003
26 Balls	Sachin Tendulkar	India v Bermuda	Port of Spain	2007
28 Balls	Tom Moody	Australia v Bangladesh	Chester-Le-Street	1999
28 Balls	Shane Watson	Australia v New Zealand	St. George's	2007
29 Balls	Arjuna Ranatunga	Sri Lanka v Kenya	Kandy	1996
29 Balls	Chris Gayle	West Indies v England	Bridgetown	2007
30 Balls	Chris Old	England v India	Lord's	1975
30 Balls	Imran Khan	Pakistan v Sri Lanka	Swansea	1983
30 Balls	Martin Crowe	New Zealand v Zimbabwe	Napier	1992
30 Balls	Sanath Jayasuriya	Sri Lanka v England	Faisalabad	1996

30 Balls	Ricardo Powell	West Indies v Bangladesh	Benoni	2003
30 Balls	John Davison	Canada v West Indies	Centurion	2003
31 Balls	Inzamam-ul-Haq	Pakistan v New Zealand	Auckland	1992
32 Balls	Sandeep Patil	India v England	Manchester	1983
32 Balls	Andrew Waller	Zimbabwe v Sri Lanka	New Plymouth	1992
32 Balls	Alec Stewart	England v Sri Lanka	Ballarat	1992
32 Balls	Mark Waugh	Australia v Zimbabwe	Hobart	1992
32 Balls	Aravinda de Silva	Sri Lanka v India	Calcutta	1996
32 Balls	Andy Blignaut	Zimbabwe v Holland	Bulawayo	2003

MOST RUNS SCORED IN AN OVER (by one batsman)

36 (6.6.6.6.6.6) Herschelle Gibbs off Daan van Bunge	South Africa v Holland	Basseterre	2007
28 (4.4.4.6.4.6) Darren Lehmann off Rudi van Vuuren	Australia v Namibia	Potchefstroom	2003
26 (4.6.4.6.6.0) Brian Lara off Barry Seebaran	West Indies v Canada	Centurion	2003

MOST SIXES IN AN INNINGS

8	Ricky Ponting	Australia v India	Johannesburg	2003
8	Imran Nazir	Pakistan v Zimbabwe	Kingston	2007

Records

Most sixes in an innings (contd.)

8	Adam Gilchrist	Australia v Sri Lanka	Bridgetown	2007
7	Vivian Richards	West Indies v Sri Lanka	Karachi	1987
7	Sourav Ganguly	India v Sri Lanka	Taunton	1999
7	Herschelle Gibbs	South Africa v Holland	Basseterre	2007
7	Brad Hodge	Australia v Holland	Basseterre	2007
7	Sanath Jayasuriya	Sri Lanka v Bangladesh	Port of Spain	2007
7	Yuvraj Singh	India v Bermuda	Port of Spain	2007
6	Kapil Dev	India v Zimbabwe	Tunbridge Wells	1983
6	David Houghton	Zimbabwe v New Zealand	Hyderabad (Ind)	1987
6	Asanka Gurusinha	Sri Lanka v Zimbabwe	Colombo	1996
6	Salim Raza	UAE v Holland	Lahore	1996
6	Scott Styris	New Zealand v Sri Lanka	Bloemfontein	2003
6	John Davison	Canada v West Indies	Centurion	2003

MOST FOURS IN AN INNINGS

21	Stephen Fleming	New Zealand v South Africa	Johannesburg	2003
19	Herschelle Gibbs	South Africa v New Zealand	Johannesburg	2003
18	Dennis Amiss	England v India	Lord's	1975

18	Craig Wishart	Zimbabwe v Namibia	Harare	2003
18	Andrew Symonds	Australia v Pakistan	Johannesburg	2003
18	Sachin Tendulkar	India v Namibia	Pietermaritzburg	2003
18	Marvan Atapattu	Sri Lanka v South Africa	Durban	2003

MOST RUNS IN BOUNDARIES IN AN INNINGS

110	(7 6s, 17 4s)	Sourav Ganguly	India v Sri Lanka	Taunton	1999
106	(7 6s, 16 4s)	Vivian Richards	West Indies v Sri Lanka	Karachi	1987
104	(8 6s, 14 4s)	Imran Nazir	Pakistan v Zimbabwe	Kingston	2007
100	(6 6s, 16 4s)	Kapil Dev	India v Zimbabwe	Tunbridge Wells	1983
100	(8 6s, 13 4s)	Adam Gilchrist	Australia v Sri Lanka	Johannesburg	2007

MOST SIXES

30	Ricky Ponting	(Australia)
28	Herschelle Gibbs	(South Africa)
27	Sanath Jayasuriya	(Sri Lanka)
25	Sourav Ganguly	(India)
23	Matthew Hayden	(Australia)
22	Vivian Richards	(West Indies)

MOST FOURS

189	Sachin Tendulkar	(India)
141	Adam Gilchrist	(Australia)
134	Stephen Fleming	(New Zealand)
130	Ricky Ponting	(Australia)
124	Brian Lara	(West Indies)
120	Sanath Jayasuriya	(Sri Lanka)
107	Aravinda de Silva	(Sri Lanka)
106	Matthew Hayden	(Australia)
106	Herschelle Gibbs	(South Africa)

HIGHEST RUN AGGREGATES IN BOUNDARIES

		Runs in boundaries	6s	4s	% of runs in boundaries
Sachin Tendulkar	(India)	870	19	189	48.44
Ricky Ponting	(Australia)	700	30	130	45.54
Adam Gilchrist	(Australia)	678	19	141	62.48
Sanath Jayasuriya	(Sri Lanka)	642	27	120	55.10
Stephen Fleming	(New Zealand)	602	11	134	56.00

HIGHEST PERCENTAGE OF RUNS IN BOUNDARIES
(minimum 300 runs)

		Runs total	Runs boundaries	6s	4s	% of runs in boundaries
John Davison	(Canada)	307	218	13	35	71.00
Mark Greatbatch	(New Zealand)	313	206	13	32	65.81
Abrahan de Villiers	(South Africa)	372	242	9	47	65.05
Adam Gilchrist	(Australia)	1085	678	19	141	62.48

HIGHEST RUN AGGREGATES IN EACH WORLD CUP

			M	I	NO	HS	Runs	Ave	100s	50s
1975	Glenn Turner	(New Zealand)	4	4	2	171*	333	166.50	2	-
1979	Gordon Greenidge	(West Indies)	4	4	1	106*	253	84.33	1	2
1983	David Gower	(England)	7	7	2	130	384	76.80	1	1
1987	Graham Gooch	(England)	8	8	-	115	471	58.87	1	3
1992	Martin Crowe	(New Zealand)	9	9	5	100*	456	114.00	1	4
1996	Sachin Tendulkar	(India)	7	7	1	137	523	87.16	2	3
1999	Rahul Dravid	(India)	8	8	1	145	461	65.85	2	3

Highest run aggregates in each World Cup (contd.)

			M	I	NO	HS	Runs	Ave	100s	50s
2003	Sachin Tendulkar	(India)	11	11	-	152	673	61.18	1	6
2007	Matthew Hayden	(Australia)	11	10	1	158	659	73.22	3	1

BATSMEN WHO HAVE CARRIED THEIR BATS THROUGH COMPLETED INNINGS

Sunil Gavaskar	36*	(132 for 3 in 60 overs)	India v England	Lord's	1975
Glenn Turner	171*	(309 for 5 in 60 overs)	New Zealand v East Africa	Birmingham	1975
Geoff Marsh	126*	(251 for 8 in 50 overs)	Australia v New Zealand	Chandigarh	1987
Andy Flower	115*	(312 for 4 in 50 overs)	Zimbabwe v Sri Lanka	New Plymouth	1992
Ramiz Raja	102*	(220 for 2 in 50 overs)	Pakistan v West Indies	Melbourne	1992
Gary Kirsten	188*	(321 for 2 in 50 overs)	South Africa v UAE	Rawalpindi	1996
Ridley Jacobs	49*	(110 all out in 46.4 overs)	West Indies v Australia	Manchester	1999
Neil Johnson	132*	(259 for 6 in 50 overs)	Zimbabwe v Australia	Lord's	1999
Craig Wishart	172*	(340 for 2 in 50 overs)	Zimbabwe v Namibia	Harare	2003
Ishwar Maraj	53*	(136 for 5 in 50 overs)	Canada v South Africa	East London	2003
Marvan Atapattu	103*	(256 for 5 in 50 overs)	Sri Lanka v Zimbabwe	East London	2003
Jeremy Bray	115*	(221 for 9 in 50 overs)	Ireland v Zimbabwe	Kingston	2007

RECORD PARTNERSHIPS FOR EACH WICKET

1st	194	Saeed Anwar & Wajahatullah Wasti	Pakistan v New Zealand	Manchester	1999
2nd	318	Sourav Ganguly & Rahul Dravid	India v Sri Lanka	Taunton	1999
3rd	237*	Rahul Dravid & Sachin Tendulkar	India v Kenya	Bristol	1999
4th	204	Michael Clarke & Brad Hodge	Australia v Holland	Basseterre	2007
5th	148	Roger Twose & Chris Cairns	New Zealand v Australia	Cardiff	1999
6th	161	Maurice Odumbe & Alpesh Vadher	Kenya v Sri Lanka	Southampton	1999
7th	98	Ramnaresh Sarwan & Ridley Jacobs	West Indies v New Zealand	Port Elizabeth	2003
8th	117	David Houghton & Iain Butchart	Zimbabwe v New Zealand	Hyderabad (I)	1987
9th	126*	Kapil Dev & Syed Kirmani	India v Zimbabwe	Tunbridge Wells	1983
10th	71	Andy Roberts & Joel Garner	West Indies v India	Manchester	1983

~ An unfinished partnership of 221 was put up by West Indies batsmen against Pakistan in 1992 but it is not a record because there were three batsmen involved. Desmond Haynes and Brian Lara put on 175 runs for the first wicket before the latter retired hurt. Then Haynes and Richie Richardson add another 46 runs.

OTHER DOUBLE CENTURY PARTNERSHIPS

2nd	244	Sachin Tendulkar & Sourav Ganguly	India v Namibia	Pietermaritzburg	2003
3rd	234*	Ricky Ponting & Damien Martyn	Australia v India	Johannesburg	2003

Records

Other double century partnerships (contd.)

2nd	228	Fieko Kloppenburg & Klaas van Noortwijk	Holland v Namibia	Bloemfontein	2003
3rd	207	Mark Waugh & Steve Waugh	Australia v Kenya	Vishakapatnam	1996
2nd	202	Sourav Ganguly & Virender Sehwag	India v Bermuda	Port of Spain	2007

MAXIMUM DUCKS

5	Ijaz Ahmed (Pakistan), Nathan Astle (New Zealand).
4	Krishnamachari Srikkanth (India), Keith Arthurton (West Indies), Inzamam-ul-Haq (Pakistan), Kyle McCallan (Ireland), Abraham de Villiers (South Africa).
3	Chris Old (England), David Houghton (Zimbabwe), Arjuna Ranatunga (Sri Lanka), Wasim Akram (Pakistan), Alistair Campbell (Zimbabwe), Javagal Srinath (India), Tim de Leede (Holland), Martin Suji (Kenya), Kennedy Otieno (Kenya), Nicholas DeGroot (Canada), Gerrie Snyman (Namibia), Mohammad Rafique (Bangladesh), Andrew Flintoff (England)

BOWLING

BEST BOWLING

7 for 15	(2.14)	Glenn McGrath	Australia v Namibia	Potchefstroom	2003
7 for 20	(2.00)	Andy Bichel	Australia v England	Port Elizabeth	2003
7 for 51	(4.86)	Winston Davis	West Indies v Australia	Leeds	1983
6 for 14	(1.17)	Gary Gilmour	Australia v England	Leeds	1975
6 for 23	(2.30)	Ashish Nehra	India v England	Durban	2003
6 for 23	(2.30)	Shane Bond	New Zealand v Australia	Port Elizabeth	2003
6 for 25	(2.73)	Chaminda Vaas	Sri Lanka v Bangladesh	Pietermaritzburg	2003
6 for 39	(3.30)	Ken MacLeay	Australia v India	Nottingham	1983

BEST BOWLING FOR THE OTHER COUNTRIES

5 for 18	(1.80)	Andrew Hall	South Africa v England	Bridgetown	2007
5 for 21	(2.17)	Paul Strang	Zimbabwe v Kenya	Patna	1996
5 for 24	(2.40)	Collins Obuya	Kenya v Sri Lanka	Nairobi	2003
5 for 27	(3.00)	Austin Codrington	Canada v Bangladesh	Durban	2003
5 for 28	(3.11)	Wasim Akram	Pakistan v Namibia	Kimberley	2003
5 for 29	(2.90)	Shaukat Dukanwala	UAE v Holland	Lahore	1996

Records

Best bowling for the other countries (contd.)

5 for 39 (3.25)	Vic Marks	England v Sri Lanka	Taunton	1983
5 for 43 (4.30)	Rudolph van Vuuren	Namibia v England	Port Elizabeth	2003
4 for 35 (3.35)	Tim de Leede	Holland v India	Paarl	2003
4 for 37 (3.70)	John Blain	Scotland v Bangladesh	Edinburgh	1999
4 for 38 (4.00)	Mashrafe Mortaza	Bangladesh v India	Port of Spain	2007
3 for 19 (3.80)	Saleem Mukuddem	Bermuda v Bangladesh	Port of Spain	2007
3 for 32 (3.55)	Boyd Rankin	Ireland v Pakistan	Kingston	2007
3 for 63 (5.25)	Zulfiqar Ali	East Africa v England	Birmingham	1975

(In brackets: Runs conceded per over)

FOUR WICKETS AND ABOVE ON WORLD CUP DEBUT

Bernard Julien	4 for 20	West Indies v Sri Lanka	Manchester	1975
Dennis Lillee	5 for 34	Australia v Pakistan	Leeds	1975
Gary Gilmour	6 for 14	Australia v England	Leeds	1975
Michael Holding	4 for 33	West Indies v India	Birmingham	1979
Duncan Fletcher	4 for 42	Zimbabwe v Australia	Nottingham	1983
Abdul Qadir	4 for 21	Pakistan v New Zealand	Birmingham	1983
Winston Davis	7 for 51	West Indies v Australia	Leeds	1983

Craig McDermott	4 for 56		Australia v India	Madras	1987
Paul Strang	4 for 40		Zimbabwe v West Indies	Hyderabad (Ind)	1996
Damien Fleming	5 for 36		Australia v India	Mumbai	1996
Allan Mullally	4 for 37		England v Sri Lanka	Lord's	1999
Neil Johnson	4 for 42		Zimbabwe v Kenya	Taunton	1999
Debashish Mohanty	4 for 56		India v Kenya	Bristol	1999
Ian Harvey	4 for 58		Australia v Pakistan	Johannesburg	2003
Austin Codrington	5 for 27		Canada v Bangladesh	Durban	2003
Ian Harvey	4 for 58		Australia v Pakistan	Johannesburg	2003
Farveez Maharoof	4 for 23		Sri Lanka v Bermuda	Port of Spain	2007

MORE THAN ONE FOUR-WICKET HAUL

Shane Warne	(Australia)	(4)	4 for 34	v Zimbabwe	Nagpur	1996
			4 for 36	v West Indies	Mohali	1996
			4 for 29	v South Africa	Birmingham	1999
			4 for 33	v Pakistan	Lord's	1999
Abdul Qadir	(Pakistan)	(3)	4 for 21	v New Zealand	Birmingham	1983
			5 for 44	v Sri Lanka	Leeds	1983
			4 for 31	v England	Rawalpindi	1987

Records

More than one four-wicket haul (contd.)

Wasim Akram	(Pakistan)	(3)	4 for 32	v New Zealand	Christchurch	1992
			4 for 40	v Australia	Leeds	1999
			5 for 28	v Namibia	Kimberley	2003
Muttiah Muralitharan (Sri Lanka)		(3)	4 for 28	v Kenya	Nairobi	2003
			4 for 19	v Ireland	St. George's	2007
			4 for 31	v New Zealand	Kingston	2007
Bernard Julien	(West Indies)	(2)	4 for 20	v Sri Lanka	Manchester	1975
			4 for 27	v New Zealand	The Oval	1975
Gary Gilmour	(Australia)	(2)	6 for 14	v England	Leeds	1975
			5 for 48	v West Indies	Lord's	1975
Bob Willis	(England)	(2)	4 for 11	v Canada	Manchester	1979
			4 for 42	v New Zealand	Birmingham	1983
Asantha de Mel	(Sri Lanka)	(2)	5 for 39	v Pakistan	Leeds	1983
			5 for 32	v New Zealand	Derby	1983
Craig McDermott	(Australia)	(2)	4 for 56	v India	Madras	1987
			5 for 44	v Pakistan	Lahore	1987
Imran Khan	(Pakistan)	(2)	4 for 37	v West Indies	Lahore	1987
			4 for 37	v England	Karachi	1987

Courtney Walsh	(West Indies)	(2)	4 for 40	v Pakistan	Lahore	1987
			4 for 25	v Bangladesh	Dublin	1999
Paul Strang	(Zimbabwe)	(2)	4 for 40	v West Indies	Hyderabad (Ind)	1996
			5 for 21	v Kenya	Patna	1996
Geoff Allott	(New Zealand)	(2)	4 for 37	v Australia	Cardiff	1999
			4 for 64	v Pakistan	Derby	1999
Allan Donald	(South Africa)	(2)	4 for 17	v England	The Oval	1999
			4 for 32	v Australia	Birmingham	1999
Lance Klusener	(South Africa)	(2)	5 for 21	v Kenya	Amsterdam	1999
			4 for 16	v Kenya	Potchefstroom	2003
Glenn McGrath	(Australia)	(2)	5 for 14	v West Indies	Manchester	1999
			7 for 15	v Namibia	Potchefstroom	2003
Javagal Srinath	(India)	(2)	4 for 30	v Holland	Paarl	2003
			4 for 35	v Sri Lanka	Johannesburg	2003
Chaminda Vaas	(Sri Lanka)	(2)	6 for 25	v Bangladesh	Pietermaritzburg	2003
			4 for 22	v West Indies	Cape Town	2003
James Anderson	(England)	(2)	4 for 25	v Holland	East London	2003
			4 for 29	v Pakistan	Cape Town	2003
Vasbert Drakes	(West Indies)	(2)	5 for 44	v Canada	Centurion	2003
			5 for 33	v Kenya	Kimberley	2003

Records

More than one four-wicket haul (contd.)

Ashish Nehra	(India)	(2)	6 for 23	v England	Durban	2003
			4 for 35	v Sri Lanka	Johannesburg	2003
Farveez Maharoof	(Sri Lanka)	(2)	4 for 23	v Bermuda	Port of Spain	2007
			4 for 25	v Ireland	St. George's	2007
Brad Hogg	(Australia)	(2)	4 for 27	v Holland	Basseterre	2007
			4 for 29	v New Zealand	St. George's	2007

Gary Gilmour, Asantha de Mel, Glenn McGrath and Vasbert Drakes are the only bowlers to capture five wickets or more in a match twice.

ONE FOUR-WICKET HAUL

Dennis Lillee (Australia)	5 for 34	v Pakistan	Leeds	1975
Tony Greig (England)	4 for 45	v New Zealand	Nottingham	1975
Sarfraz Nawaz (Pakistan)	4 for 44	v West Indies	Birmingham	1975
John Snow (England)	4 for 11	v East Africa	Birmingham	1975
Keith Boyce (West Indies)	4 for 50	v Australia	Lord's	1975
Michael Holding (West Indies)	4 for 33	v India	Birmingham	1979
Chris Old (England)	4 for 08	v Canada	Manchester	1979
Mike Hendrick (England)	4 for 15	v Pakistan	Leeds	1979

Alan Hurst (Australia)	5 for 21	v Canada	Birmingham	1979
Asif Iqbal (Pakistan)	4 for 56	v West Indies	The Oval	1979
Joel Garner (West Indies)	5 for 38	v England	Lord's	1979
Duncan Fletcher (Zimbabwe)	4 for 42	v Australia	Nottingham	1983
Graham Dilley (England)	4 for 45	v Sri Lanka	Taunton	1983
Vic Marks (England)	5 for 39	v Sri Lanka	Taunton	1983
Winston Davis (West Indies)	7 for 51	v Australia	Leeds	1983
Richard Hadlee (New Zealand)	5 for 25	v Sri Lanka	Bristol	1983
Kapil Dev (India)	5 for 43	v Australia	Nottingham	1983
Ken MacLeay (Australia)	6 for 39	v India	Nottingham	1983
Madan Lal (India)	4 for 20	v Australia	Chelmsford	1983
Roger Binny (India)	4 for 29	v Australia	Chelmsford	1983
Simon O'Donnell (Australia)	4 for 39	v Zimbabwe	Madras	1987
Manoj Prabhakar (India)	for 19	v Zimbabwe	Bombay	1987
Eddie Hemmings (England)	4 for 52	v India	Bombay	1987
Meyrick Pringle (South Africa)	4 for 11	v West Indies	Christchurch	1992
Ian Botham (England)	4 for 31	v Australia	Sydney	1992
Chris Lewis (England)	4 for 30	v Sri Lanka	Ballarat	1992

One four-wicket haul (contd.)

Anderson Cummins (West Indies)	4 for 33	v India	Wellington	1992
Chandika Hathurusinghe (Sri Lanka)	4 for 57	v West Indies	Berri	1992
Eddo Brandes (Zimbabwe)	4 for 21	v England	Albury	1992
Mike Whitney (Australia)	4 for 34	v West Indies	Melbourne	1992
Waqar Younis (Pakistan)	4 for 26	v Holland	Lahore	1996
Damien Fleming (Australia)	5 for 36	v India	Mumbai	1996
Shaukat Dukanwala (UAE)	5 for 29	v Holland	Lahore	1996
Roger Harper (West Indies)	4 for 47	v South Africa	Karachi	1996
Allan Mullally (England)	4 for 37	v Sri Lanka	Lord's	1999
Neil Johnson (Zimbabwe)	4 for 42	v Kenya	Taunton	1999
Darren Gough (England)	4 for 34	v Kenya	Canterbury	1999
Debashish Mohanty (India)	4 for 56	v Kenya	Bristol	1999
Mervyn Dillon (West Indies)	4 for 46	v New Zealand	Southampton	1999
John Blain (Scotland)	4 for 37	v Bangladesh	Edinburgh	1999
Robin Singh (India)	5 for 31	v Sri Lanka	Taunton	1999
Saqlain Mushtaq (Pakistan)	5 for 35	v Bangladesh	Northampton	1999
Chris Harris (New Zealand)	4 for 07	v Scotland	Edinburgh	1999

Venkatesh Prasad (India)	5 for 27	v Pakistan	Manchester	1999
Shaun Pollock (South Africa)	5 for 36	v Australia	Birmingham	1999
Ian Harvey (Australia)	4 for 58	v Pakistan	Johannesburg	2003
Austin Codrington (Canada)	5 for 27	v Bangladesh	Durban	2003
Tim de Leede (Holland)	4 for 35	v India	Paarl	2003
Anil Kumble (India)	4 for 32	v Holland	Paarl	2003
Andre Adams (New Zealand)	4 for 44	v West Indies	Port Elizabeth	2003
Thomas Odoyo (Kenya)	4 for 28	v Canada	Cape Town	2003
Shoaib Akhtar (Pakistan)	4 for 46	v Namibia	Kimberley	2003
Rudolph van Vuuren (Namibia)	5 for 43	v England	Port Elizabeth	2003
Prabath Nissanka (Sri Lanka)	4 for 12	v Canada	Paarl	2003
Makhaya Ntini (South Africa)	4 for 24	v Bangladesh	Bloemfontein	2003
Yuvraj Singh (India)	4 for 06	v Namibia	Pietermaritzburg	2003
Collins Obuya (Kenya)	5 for 24	v Sri Lanka	Nairobi	2003
Maurice Odumbe (Kenya)	4 for 38	v Bangladesh	Johannesburg	2003
Andy Bichel (Australia)	7 for 20	v England	Port Elizabeth	2003
Andrew Caddick (England)	4 for 35	v Australia	Port Elizabeth	2003
Feiko Kloppenburg (Holland)	4 for 42	v Namibia	Bloemfontein	2003

Records

One four-wicket haul (contd.)

Adeel Raja (Holland)	4 for 42	v Namibia	Bloemfontein	2003
Jacob Oram (New Zealand)	4 for 52	v Canada	Benoni	2003
Shane Bond (New Zealand)	6 for 23	v Australia	Port Elizabeth	2003
Brett Lee (Australia)	5 for 42	v New Zealand	Port Elizabeth	2003
Zaheer Khan (India)	4 for 42	v New Zealand	Centurion	2003
Mashrafe Mortaza (Bangladesh)	4 for 38	v India	Port of Spain	2007
Charl Langeveldt (South Africa)	5 for 39	v Sri Lanka	Providence	2007
Lasith Malinga (Sri Lanka)	4 for 54	v South Africa	Providence	2007
Andrew Flintoff (England)	4 for 43	v Ireland	Providence	2007
Scott Styris (New Zealand)	4 for 43	v Bangladesh	North Sound	2007
Sajid Mahmood (England)	4 for 50	v Sri Lanka	North Sound	2007
Andre Nel (South Africa)	5 for 45	v Bangladesh	Providence	2007
Daniel Vettori (New Zealand)	4 for 23	v Ireland	Providence	2007
Nathan Bracken (Australia)	4 for 19	v Sri Lanka	St. George's	2007
Andrew Hall (South Africa)	5 for 18	v England	Bridgetown	2007
Shaun Tait (Australia)	4 for 39	v South Africa	Gros Islet	2007

There have been 128 four-wicket plus haul by 100 bowlers

FOUR-WICKET HAULS IN CONSECUTIVE MATCHES

Gary Gilmour	(Australia)	6 for 14	v England, Leeds	&	5 for 48	v West Indies, Lord's	1975
Asantha de Mel	(Sri Lanka)	5 for 39	v Pakistan, Leeds	&	5 for 32	v New Zealand, Derby	1983
Imran Khan	(Pakistan)	4 for 37	v West Indies, Lahore	&	4 for 37	v England, Karachi	1987
Shane Warne	(Australia)	4 for 29	v South Africa, Birmingham	&	4 for 33	v Pakistan, Lord's	1999
Muttiah Muralitharan	(Sri Lanka)	4 for 19	v Ireland, St. George's	&	4 for 31	v New Zealand, Kingston	2007

FOUR-WICKET HAULS IN THE SAME INNINGS

Bob Willis	4 for 11	&	Chris Old	4 for 08	England v Canada	Manchester	1979
Graham Dilley	4 for 45	&	Vic Marks	5 for 39	England v Sri Lanka	Taunton	1983
Madan Lal	4 for 20	&	Roger Binny	4 for 29	India v Australia	Chelmsford	1983
Shaun Pollock	5 for 36	&	Allan Donald	4 for 32	South Africa v Australia	Birmingham	1999
Javagal Srinath	4 for 30	&	Anil Kumble	4 for 32	India v Holland	Paarl	2003
Wasim Akram	5 for 28	&	Shoaib Akhtar	4 for 46	Pakistan v Namibia	Kimberley	2003
Feiko Kloppenburg	4 for 42	&	Adeel Raja	4 for 42	Holland v Namibia	Bloemfontein	2003
Javagal Srinath	4 for 35	&	Ashish Nehra	4 for 35	India v Sri Lanka	Johannesburg	2003
Farveez Maharoof	4 for 25	&	Muttiah Muralitharan	4 for 19	Sri Lanka v Ireland	St. George's	2007

HAT TRICK

Chetan Sharma	India v New Zealand at Nagpur, 1987 Victim – all bowled: Ken Rutherford, Ian Smith and Ewan Chatfield, off the 4th, 5th and 6th balls of his sixth over. His final figures were 10-2-51-3.
Saqlain Mushtaq	Pakistan v Zimbabwe at The Oval, London, 1999 Victims: Henry Olonga stumped Moin Khan, Adam Huckle stumped Moin Khan, and Mpumelelo Mbangwa lbw, off the first three balls of his seventh over. His final figures were 6.3-1-16-3.
Chaminda Vaas	Sri Lanka v Bangladesh at Pietermaritzburg, 2003 Victims: Hannan Sarkar bowled, Mohammad Ashraful caught & bowled, and Ehsanul Haque caught Jayawardene, off the first three balls of the first over of the match. He also took a fourth wicket, of Sanwar Hossain, in that over. His final figures were 9.1-2-25-6.
Brett Lee	Australia v Kenya at Durban, 2003 Victims: Kennedy Otieno bowled, Brijal Patel caught Ponting, and David Obuya bowled, off the 4th, 5th and 6th balls of his second over. His final figures were 8-3-14-3.
Lasith Malinga	Sri Lanka v South Africa at Providence, 2007 Victims: Shaun Pollock bowled, Andrew Hall caught Tharanga, Jacques Kallis caught Sangakkara, and Makhaya Ntini bowled, off the 5th and 6th balls of his eighth over and 1st and 2nd balls of his ninth over. This is the only instance of four wickets being taken off four successive deliveries. His final figures were 9.2-0-54-4.

WICKET OFF FIRST BALL IN THE WORLD CUP

Mark Ealham	England v Sri Lanka	Lord's	1999
Ian Harvey	Australia v Pakistan	Johannesburg	2003
Mohammad Yousuf	Pakistan v Zimbabwe	Kingston	2007

This is Yousuf's only delivery in the World Cup.

HIGHEST WICKET AGGREGATES IN EACH WORLD CUP

		Balls	Mdn	Runs	Wkts	Ave	BB	RO
1975	Gary Gilmour (Australia)	144	8	62	11	5.63	6/14	2.58
1979	Mike Hendrick (England)	336	14	149	10	14.90	4/15	2.66
1983	Roger Binny (India)	528	9	336	18	18.66	4/29	3.81
1987	Craig McDermott (Australia)	438	3	341	18	18.94	5/44	4.67
1992	Wasim Akram (Pakistan)	538	3	338	18	18.77	4/32	3.76
1996	Anil Kumble (India)	418	3	281	15	18.73	3/28	4.03
1999	Geoff Allott (New Zealand)	526	7	325	20	16.25	4/37	3.70
	Shane Warne (Australia)	566	13	361	20	18.05	4/29	3.82
2003	Chaminda Vaas (Sri Lanka)	528	14	331	23	14.39	6/25	3.76
2007	Glenn McGrath (Australia)	485	5	357	26	13.73	3/14	4.41

BEST STRIKE RATES – DELIVERIES PER WICKET
(minimum 15 wickets)

		Balls	Mdns	Runs	Wkts	Ave	Best	SR
Vasbert Drakes	(West Indies)	311	7	208	16	13.00	5/33	19.43
Lasith Malinga	(Sri Lanka)	350	6	284	18	15.77	4/54	19.44
Andy Bichel	(Australia)	342	7	197	16	12.31	7/20	21.37
Shaun Tait	(Australia)	507	1	467	23	20.30	4/39	22.04
Brett Lee	(Australia)	499	9	394	22	17.90	5/42	22.68
Shoaib Akhtar	(Pakistan)	749	8	644	27	23.85	4/46	23.81
Waqar Younis	(Pakistan)	559	7	466	22	21.18	4/26	25.40
Geoff Allott	(New Zealand)	526	7	325	20	16.25	4/37	26.30
Patrick Patterson	(West Indies)	396	2	278	15	18.53	3/31	26.40
Nathan Bracken	(Australia)	430	10	258	16	16.12	4/19	26.87
Lance Klusener	(South Africa)	605	7	487	22	22.13	5/21	27.50
Glenn McGrath	(Australia)	1955	42	1292	71	18.19	7/15	27.53
Ashish Nehra	(India)	415	9	289	15	19.26	6/23	27.66
Brad Hogg	(Australia)	951	10	654	34	19.23	4/27	27.97
Saqlain Mushtaq	(Pakistan)	674	7	494	23	21.47	5/35	29.30

Shane Bond	(New Zealand)	886	21	518	30	17.26	6/23	29.53
Imran Khan	(Pakistan)	1017	18	655	34	19.26	4/37	29.91

BEST ECONOMY RATES – RUNS CONCEDED PER OVER (minimum 15 wickets)

		Balls	Mdns	Runs	Wkts	Ave	Best	RO
Bob Willis	(England)	709	27	315	18	17.50	4/11	2.66
Chris Old	(England)	543	18	243	16	15.18	4/08	2.68
Richard Hadlee	(New Zealand)	877	38	421	22	19.13	5/25	2.88
Michael Holding	(West Indies)	695	16	341	20	17.05	4/33	2.94
Curtly Ambrose	(West Indies)	987	20	499	24	20.79	3/28	3.03
Andy Roberts	(West Indies)	1021	29	552	26	21.23	3/32	3.24
Ian Botham	(England)	1332	33	762	30	25.40	4/31	3.43
Andy Bichel	(Australia)	342	7	197	16	12.31	7/20	3.45
Courtney Walsh	(West Indies)	948	23	547	27	20.25	4/25	3.46
Shane Bond	(New Zealand)	886	21	518	30	17.26	6/23	3.50
Gavin Larsen	(New Zealand)	1020	12	599	18	33.27	3/16	3.52
John Traicos	(Zimbabwe)	1128	13	673	16	42.06	3/35	3.57
Shaun Pollock	(South Africa)	1614	37	970	31	31.29	5/36	3.60

Best economy rates (contd.)

		Balls	Mdns	Runs	Wkts	Ave	Best	RO
Nathan Bracken	(Australia)	430	10	258	16	16.12	4/19	3.60
Sarfraz Nawaz	(Pakistan)	714	15	435	16	27.18	4/44	3.65
Madan Lal	(India)	698	12	426	22	19.36	4/20	3.66
Roger Harper	(West Indies)	792	10	488	18	27.11	4/47	3.69
Geoff Allott	(New Zealand)	526	7	325	20	16.25	4/37	3.70
Abdul Qadir	(Pakistan)	814	8	506	24	21.08	5/44	3.72
Brian McMillan	(South Africa)	696	12	433	17	25.47	3/11	3.73
Kapil Dev	(India)	1422	27	892	28	31.85	5/43	3.76
Muttiah Muralitharan	(Sri Lanka)	1635	14	1044	53	19.69	4/19	3.83
Shane Warne	(Australia)	977	16	624	32	19.50	4/29	3.83
Imran Khan	(Pakistan)	1017	18	655	34	19.26	4/37	3.86
Mohinder Amarnath	(India)	663	9	431	16	26.93	3/12	3.90
Shane Bond	(New Zealand)	468	12	305	17	17.94	6/23	3.91
Andrew Flintoff	(England)	814	12	534	23	23.21	4/43	3.93
Philip DeFreitas	(England)	1127	30	742	29	25.58	3/28	3.95
Glenn McGrath	(Australia)	1955	42	1292	71	18.19	7/15	3.96
Chaminda Vaas	(Sri Lanka)	1570	39	1040	49	21.22	6/25	3.97

MOST ECONOMICAL BOWLING ANALYSIS
(minimum 5 overs)

	O	M	R	W	RO			
Dermot Reeve	5	3	2	1	0.40	England v Pakistan	Adelaide	1992
Bishan Singh Bedi	12	8	6	1	0.50	India v East Africa	Leeds	1975
Andre Botha	8	4	5	2	0.62	Ireland v Pakistan	Kingston	2007
Mike Hendrick	8	4	5	1	0.62	England v Canada	Manchester	1979
Shaun Pollock	6	3	4	1	0.66	South Africa v Holland	Basseterre	2007
Barry Wood	5	2	4	0	0.80	England v India	Lord's	1975
Chris Old	10	5	8	4	0.80	England v Canada	Manchester	1979
Curtly Ambrose	10	4	8	2	0.80	West Indies v Scotland	Leicester	1999
Richard Hadlee	12	6	10	0	0.83	New Zealand v East Africa	Birmingham	1975
Asif Karim	8.2	6	7	3	0.84	Kenya v Australia	Durban	2003
John Snow	12	6	11	4	0.91	England v East Africa	Birmingham	1975
Somchandra de Silva	12	5	11	2	0.91	Sri Lanka v New Zealand	Derby	1983
Derek Pringle	8.2	5	8	3	0.96	England v Pakistan	Adelaide	1992
Wasim Raja	7	4	7	1	1.00	Pakistan v Sri Lanka	Nottingham	1975
Majid Khan	11	4	11	1	1.00	Pakistan v Canada	Leeds	1979

Records

Most economical bowling analysis (contd.)

	O	M	R	W	RO			
Bob Willis	9	4	9	1	1.00	England v Sri Lanka	Leeds	1983
Courtney Walsh	7	1	7	3	1.00	West Indies v Scotland	Leicester	1999

MOST EXPENSIVE BOWLING ANALYSIS
(minimum 5 overs)

	O	M	R	W	RO			
Devon Smith	5	0	56	2	11.20	West Indies v South Africa	St. George's	2007
Rajab Ali	6	0	67	0	11.16	Kenya v Sri Lanka	Kandy	1996
Mark Gillespie	6	0	67	0	11.16	New Zealand v Australia	St. George's	2007
Andre Adams	5	0	54	1	10.80	New Zealand v Zimbabwe	Bloemfontein	2003
Malachi Jones	7	0	74	1	10.57	Bermuda v India	Port of Spain	2007
Liam Plunkett	7	0	71	1	10.14	England v West Indies	Bridgetown	2007

MOST RUNS CONCEDED IN AN OVER

36	Daan van Bunge (6 sixes)	Holland v South Africa	Basseterre	2007
30	Luuk van Troost (includes 4 wides)	Holland v South Africa	Basseterre	2007
28	Rudi van Vuuren	Namibia v Australia	Potchefstroom	2003

26	Barry Seebaran	Canada v West Indies	Centurion	2003
26	Darren Powell	West Indies v South Africa	St. George's	2007
24	Chris Cairns (includes a no-ball)	New Zealand v South Africa	Birmingham	1999
23	Martin Crowe (New Zealand), Vinodhan John (Sri Lanka), Ravi Ratnayeke (Sri Lanka), Sachin Tendulkar (India) and Shaun Pollock.			

ALL ROUND

OUTSTANDING ALLROUND PERFORMANCES
(minimum 30 runs & 3 wickets in a match)

Keith Boyce	34 & 4/50	West Indies v Australia	Lord's	1975
Majid Khan	61 & 3/53	Pakistan v Australia	Nottingham	1979
Vivian Richards	42 & 3/52	West Indies v Pakistan	The Oval	1979
Duncan Fletcher	69* & 4/42	Zimbabwe v Australia	Nottingham	1983
Abdul Qadir	4/21 & 41*	Pakistan v New Zealand	Birmingham	1983
Jeremy Coney	33 & 3/28	New Zealand v Pakistan	Birmingham	1983
Kapil Dev	5/43 & 40	India v Australia	Nottingham	1983
Richard Hadlee	3/32 & 31	New Zealand v England	Birmingham	1983

Records

Outstanding allround performances *(contd.)*

Kevin Curran	3/65 & 73	Zimbabwe v India	Tunbridge Wells	1983
Mohammad Azharuddin	54* & 3/19	India v Australia	New Delhi	1987
Imran Khan	3/36 & 58	Pakistan v Australia	Lahore	1987
Iain Butchart	3/57 & 33	Zimbabwe v Pakistan	Hobart	1992
Ian Botham	4/31 & 53	England v Australia	Sydney	1992
Peter Kirsten	3/31 & 62*	South Africa v Zimbabwe	Canberra	1992
Wasim Akram	33 & 3/49	Pakistan v England	Melbourne	1992
Shane Thomson	31* & 3/20	New Zealand v UAE	Faisalabad	1996
Mark Waugh	30 & 3/38	Australia v West Indies	Jaipur	1996
Aravinda de Silva	3/42 & 107*	Sri Lanka v Australia	Lahore	1996
Neil Johnson	4/42 & 59	Zimbabwe v Kenya	Taunton	1999
Azhar Mahmood	37 & 3/48	Pakistan v West Indies	Bristol	1999
Lance Klusener	52* & 3/21	South Africa v Sri Lanka	Northampton	1999
Wasim Akram	37* & 3/23	Pakistan v Scotland	Chester-Le-Street	1999
Tom Moody	3/25 & 56*	Australia v Bangladesh	Chester-Le-Street	1999
Neil Johnson	76 & 3/27	Zimbabwe v South Africa	Chelmsford	1999
Sourav Ganguly	40 and 3/27	India v England	Birmingham	1999

Wasim Akram	3/64 & 33	Pakistan v Australia	Johannesburg	2003
Andre Adams	35* & 4/44	New Zealand v West Indies	Port Elizabeth	2003
John Davison	31 & 3/15	Canada v Kenya	Cape Town	2003
Maurice Odumbe	52* & 4/38	Kenya v Bangladesh	Johannesburg	2003
Andy Bichel	7/20 & 34*	Australia v England	Port Elizabeth	2003
Feiko Kloppenburg	121 & 4/42	Holland v Namibia	Bloemfontein	2003
John Davison	75 & 3/61	Canada v New Zealand	Benoni	2003
Dwayne Smith	32 & 3/36	West Indies v Pakistan	Kingston	2007
Sunil Dhaniram	3/41 & 30	Canada v England	Gros Islet	2007
Andrew Flintoff	43 & 4/43	England v Ireland	Providence	2007
Sanath Jayasuriya	115 & 3/38	Sri Lanka v West Indies	Providence	2007
Craig McMillan	3/23 & 38*	New Zealand v South Africa	St. George's	2007
Michael Vaughan	3/39 & 79	England v West Indies	Bridgetown	2007

WICKETKEEPING

MOST DISMISSALS

Adam Gilchrist (Australia)	52	(45 catches, 7 stumpings)
Kumar Sangakkara (Sri Lanka)	32	(26 catches, 6 stumpings)
Mark Boucher (South Africa)	31	(31 catches)
Moin Khan (Pakistan)	30	(23 catches, 7 stumpings)
Alec Stewart (England)	23	(21 catches, 2 stumpings)
Brendon McCullum (New Zealand)	23	(22 catches, 1 stumping)
Wasim Bari (Pakistan)	22	(18 catches, 4 stumpings)
Ridley Jacobs (West Indies)	22	(21 catches, 1 stumping)
Ian Healy (Australia)	21	(18 catches, 3 stumpings)
Jeff Dujon (West Indies)	20	(19 catches, 1 stumping)
Rodney Marsh (Australia)	18	(17 catches, 1 stumping)
Kiran More (India)	18	(12 catches, 6 stumpings)
Rashid Latif (Pakistan)	17	(14 catches, 3 stumpings)
Deryck Murray (West Indies)	16	(16 catches)
Nayan Mongia (India)	16	(12 catches, 4 stumpings)

Rahul Dravid (India)	16 (15 catches, 1 stumping)
David Richardson (South Africa)	15 (14 catches, 1 stumping)
Kennedy Otieno (Kenya)	15 (11 catches, 4 stumpings)

MOST CATCHES BY A WICKETKEEPER

45	Adam Gilchrist (Australia)
31	Mark Boucher (South Africa)
26	Kumar Sangakkara (Sri Lanka)
23	Moin Khan (Pakistan)
22	Brendon McCullum (New Zealand)
21	Alec Stewart (England)
21	Ridley Jacobs (West Indies)

MOST STUMPINGS

7	Moin Khan (Pakistan)
7	Adam Gilchrist (Australia)
6	Kiran More (India)
6	Kumar Sangakkara (Sri Lanka)

MOST DISMISSALS IN A MATCH

Adam Gilchrist (Australia)	6 (6 ct)	v Namibia	Potchefstroom	2003
Syed Kirmani (India)	5 (5 ct)	v Zimbabwe	Leicester	1983
Jimmy Adams (West Indies)	5 (4 ct, 1 st)	v Kenya	Pune	1996
Rashid Latif (Pakistan)	5 (4 ct, 1 st)	v New Zealand	Lahore	1996
Nayan Mongia (India)	5 (4 ct, 1 st)	v Zimbabwe	Leicester	1999
Ridley Jacobs (West Indies)	5 (5 ct)	v New Zealand	Southampton	1999

MOST CATCHES BY A WICKETKEEPER IN A MATCH

6	Adam Gilchrist	Australia v Namibia	Potchefstroom	2003
5	Syed Kirmani	India v Zimbabwe	Leicester	1983
5	Ridley Jacobs	West Indies v New Zealand	Southampton	1999

MOST STUMPINGS IN A MATCH

2	Syed Kirmani	India v West Indies	Manchester	1983
2	Wasim Bari	Pakistan v Sri Lanka	Leeds	1983
2	Kiran More	India v Zimbabwe	Bombay	1987
2	Khaled Mashud	Bangladesh v Australia	Chester-Le-Street	1999

2	Moin Khan	Pakistan v Bangladesh	Northampton	1999
2	Moin Khan	Pakistan v Zimbabwe	The Oval	1999
2	Kennedy Otieno	Kenya v Bangladesh	Johannesburg	2003
2	Mahendra Singh Dhoni	India v Bangladesh	Port of Spain	2007
2	Kumar Sangakkara	Sri Lanka v South Africa	Providence	2007
2	Kumar Sangakkara	Sri Lanka v West Indies	Providence	2007

MOST DISMISSALS IN EACH WORLD CUP

		M	Dis	Ct	St
1975	Rodney Marsh (Australia)	5	10	9	1
1979	Deryck Murray (West Indies)	4	7	7	-
	Wasim Bari (Pakistan)	4	7	6	1
1983	Jeff Dujon (West Indies)	8	16	15	1
1987	Kiran More (India)	6	11	6	5
	Greg Dyer (Australia)	8	11	9	2
1992	David Richardson (South Africa)	9	15	14	1
1996	Ian Healy (Australia)	7	12	9	3
1999	Moin Khan (Pakistan)	10	16	12	4

Most dismissals in each World Cup (contd.)

		M	Dis	Ct	St
2003	Adam Gilchrist (Australia)	10	21	21	-
2007	Adam Gilchrist (Australia)	11	17	12	5

HIGHEST TOTAL WITH NO BYE CONCEDED

413 for 5 (50 overs)	Dean Minors	Bermuda v India	Port of Spain	2007
377 for 6 (50 overs)	Mark Boucher	South Africa v Australia	Basseterre	2007
373 for 6 (50 overs)	Romesh Kaluwitharana	Sri Lanka v India	Taunton	1999

HIGHEST SCORE BY A WICKETKEEPER

149	Adam Gilchrist	Australia v Sri Lanka	Bridgetown	2007
145	Rahul Dravid	India v Sri Lanka	Taunton	1999
142	David Houghton	Zimbabwe v New Zealand	Hyderabad (Ind)	1987
115*	Andy Flower	Zimbabwe v Sri Lanka	New Plymouth	1992

WICKETKEEPER'S DOUBLE
(minimum 3 dismissals & 30 runs in a match)

Deryck Murray	4 ct & 30*	West Indies v Sri Lanka	Manchester	1975

Rodney Marsh	3 ct & 50*	Australia v Zimbabwe	Nottingham	1983
Wasim Bari	3 ct/1st & 34	Pakistan v New Zealand	Birmingham	1983
David Williams	32* & 4 ct	West Indies v New Zealand	Auckland	1992
Alec Stewart	3 ct & 88	England v Sri Lanka	Lord's	1999
Moin Khan	47 & 3 ct	Pakistan v Scotland	Chester-le-Street	1999
Ridley Jacobs	5 ct & 80*	West Indies v New Zealand	Southampton	1999
Adam Gilchrist	31 & 4 ct	Australia v India	The Oval	1999
Alec Stewart	30 & 3 ct	England v Pakistan	Cape Town	2003
Rahul Dravid	62 & 3 ct	India v England	Durban	2003
Kumar Sangakkara	3 ct/1st & 39*	Sri Lanka v Australia	Port Elizabeth	2003
Kumar Sangakkara	76 & 3 ct	Sri Lanka v Bermuda	Port of Spain	2007
Adam Gilchrist	149 & 2 ct/1st	Australia v Sri Lanka	Bridgetown	2007

FIELDING

MOST CATCHES BY A FIELDER

		Matches	Catches
Ricky Ponting	(Australia)	39	25
Sanath Jayasuriya	(Sri Lanka)	38	18
Chris Cairns	(New Zealand)	28	16
Brian Lara	(West Indies)	34	16
Inzamam-ul-Haq	(Pakistan)	35	16
Anil Kumble	(India)	18	14
Steve Waugh	(Australia)	33	14
Aravinda de Silva	(Sri Lanka)	35	14
Carl Hooper	(West Indies)	20	13
Paul Collingwood	(England)	14	12
Clive Lloyd	(West Indies)	17	12
Graeme Hick	(England)	20	12
Desmond Haynes	(West Indies)	25	12
Kapil Dev	(India)	26	12

Shaun Pollock	(South Africa)	31	12
Muttiah Muralitharan	(Sri Lanka)	31	12
Stephen Fleming	(New Zealand)	33	12
Graham Thorpe	(England)	11	11
Daryll Cullinan	(South Africa)	15	11
Mark Waugh	(Australia)	22	11
Ijaz Ahmed	(Pakistan)	29	11
Mohammad Azharuddin	(India)	30	11
Graeme Smith	(South Africa)	13	10
Scott Styris	(New Zealand)	18	10
Alistair Campbell	(Zimbabwe)	19	10
Ian Botham	(England)	22	10
Hansie Cronje	(South Africa)	23	10
Steve Tikolo	(Kenya)	23	10
Allan Border	(Australia)	25	10
Herschelle Gibbs	(South Africa)	25	10
Javed Miandad	(Pakistan)	33	10
Sachin Tendulkar	(Pakistan)	36	10

Note: In addition, Javed Miandad effected 1 stumping as substitute wicketkeeper in the semi-final against Australia in 1987.

MOST CATCHES BY A FIELDER IN A MATCH

Mohammad Kaif	4	India v Sri Lanka	Johannesburg	2003
Clive Lloyd	3	West Indies v Sri Lanka	Manchester	1975
Dermot Reeve	3	England v Pakistan	Adelaide	1992
Ijaz Ahmed	3	Pakistan v Australia	Perth	1992
Allan Border	3	Australia v Zimbabwe	Hobart	1992
Chris Cairns	3	New Zealand v UAE	Faisalabad	1996
Graham Thorpe	3	England v Sri Lanka	Lord's	1999
Nathan Astle	3	New Zealand v Australia	Cardiff	1999
Iain Philip	3	Scotland v Bangladesh	Edinburgh	1999
Ricky Ponting	3	Australia v Bangladesh	Chester-Le-Street	1999
Stuart Williams	3	West Indies v Scotland	Leicester	1999
Andy Whittal	3	Zimbabwe v South Africa	Chelmsford	1999
Virender Sehwag	3	India v Holland	Paarl	2003
Louis Burger	3	Namibia v England	Port Elizabeth	2003
Boeta Dippenaar	3	South Africa v Bangladesh	Bloemfontein	2003
Dinesh Mongia	3	India v Namibia	Pietermaritzburg	2003

Virender Sehwag	3	India v England	Durban	2003
Ashley Giles	3	England v Australia	Port Elizabeth	2003
Steve Tikolo	3	Kenya v New Zealand	Gros Islet	2007
Inzamam-ul-Haq	3	Pakistan v Zimbabwe	Kingston	2007
Eoin Morgan	3	Ireland v New Zealand	Providence	2007
Chamara Silva	3	New Zealand v Sri Lanka	St. George's	2007

Virender Sehwag is the only fielder who has taken three catches in a match twice

MOST CATCHES BY A FIELDER IN EACH WORLD CUP

			Matches	Catches
1975	Clive Lloyd	(West Indies)	5	4
1979	Asif Iqbal	(Pakistan)	4	4
	Alvin Kallicharan	(West Indies)	4	4
	Mike Brearley	(England)	5	4
1983	Kapil Dev	(India)	8	7
1987	Kapil Dev	(India)	7	5
1992	Kepler Wessels	(South Africa)	9	7
1996	Anil Kumble	(India)	7	8

Most catches by a fielder in each World Cup (contd.)

			Matches	Catches
1999	Daryll Cullinan	(South Africa)	9	8
2003	Ricky Ponting	(Australia)	11	11
2007	Paul Collingwood	(England)	9	8
	Graeme Smith	(South Africa)	10	8

MISCELLANEOUS

MOST APPEARANCES

39	Ricky Ponting (Australia), Glenn McGrath (Australia)
38	Wasim Akram (Pakistan), Sanath Jayasuriya (Sri Lanka)
36	Sachin Tendulkar (India)
35	Aravinda de Silva (Sri Lanka), Inzamam-ul-Haq (Pakistan)
34	Javagal Srinath (India), Brian Lara (West Indies)
33	Javed Miandad (Pakistan), Steve Waugh (Australia), Stephen Fleming (New Zealand)
30	Arjuna Ranatunga (Sri Lanka), Mohammad Azharuddin (India), Andy Flower (Zimbabwe)

MOST APPEARANCES IN WORLD CUP WINNING TEAMS (FINAL)

3	Ricky Ponting, Glenn McGrath, and Adam Gilchrist (all Australia)	1999, 2003 & 2007
2	Clive Lloyd, Gordon Greenidge, Alvin Kallicharan, Vivian Richards, Deryck Murray and Andy Roberts (all West Indies)	1975 & 1979
2	Steve Waugh (Australia)	1987 & 1999
2	Michael Bevan and Darren Lehmann (all Australia)	1999 & 2003
2	Matthew Hayden, Andrew Symonds and Brad Hogg (all Australia)	2003 & 2007

CAPTAINED IN HIGHEST NUMBER OF MATCHES

27	Stephen Fleming	(New Zealand)	1999-2007
23	Mohammad Azharuddin	(India)	1992-1999
22	Imran Khan	(Pakistan)	1983-1992
22	Ricky Ponting	(Australia)	2003-2007

MOST MAN-OF-THE-MATCH AWARDS

8	Sachin Tendulkar	(India)
5	Vivian Richards	(West Indies)
5	Graham Gooch	(England)

Most man-of-the-match awards (contd.)

5	Lance Klusener	(South Africa)	
5	Sanath Jayasuriya	(Sri Lanka)	
5	Glenn McGrath	(Australia)	

MOST MAN-OF-THE-MATCH AWARDS IN A SINGLE WORLD CUP

4	Aravinda de Silva	(Sri Lanka)	1996
4	Lance Klusener	(South Africa)	1999

MOST CONSECUTIVE MAN-OF-THE-MATCH AWARDS

3	Graham Gooch	(England)	1987
3	Lance Klusener	(South Africa)	1999

MAN-OF-THE-MATCH AWARDS IN SEMI-FINAL AND FINAL OF THE SAME WORLD CUP

Mohinder Amarnath	(India)	1983
Aravinda de Silva	(Sri Lanka)	1996
Shane Warne	(Australia)	1999

Bibliography

Books

Indian Cricket, Kasturi & Sons, Chennai, many editions.
Wisden Cricketers' Almanack, John Wisden & Co., Guildford, Surrey, many editions.
Peter A. Murray & Qamar Ahmed, *World Cup Cricket 1983,* Wide World of Sport Publications, Sydney, 1983.
Charanpal Singh Sobti, *World Cup Cricket*, Rupa & Co., Calcutta, 1992.
Dr. Narottam Puri, *World Cup 1996*, Indus, New Delhi, 1996.
Bruce Smith, Mark Webb & Salim Parvez, *Cricket World Cup 1999*, Collins Willow, London, 1999.
Rajesh Kumar & Indra Vikram Singh, *Peter Murray's World Cup Cricket*, Rupa & Co., New Delhi, 2002.

Magazines / Dailies

Barclay's World of Cricket (United Kingdom)
Cricket Samrat (India)
Cricket World (India)
Cricketer International (United Kingdom)
The Hindu (India)
The Illustrated Weekly of India (India)
India Today (India)
Outlook (India)
Sportsweek (India)

Bibliography

Sportsweek Cricket Quarterly (India)
Sportsworld (India)
The Sportstar (India)
Sunday (India)
The Sunday Telegraph (United Kingdom)
The Telegraph (United Kingdom)
The Times of India (India)
Wisden Asia Cricket (India)
Wisden Cricket Monthly (United Kingdom)

Websites

cricinfo.com
icccricketworldcup.com
news.caribseek.com
wisden.com